— A —
GERMAN
POW
in New Mexico

4. 6. 05

To Capt. Walter F Baker
Remembering Las Cruces
with Fondress
With the best wishes
            Walter Schmid

—A—

GERMAN POW

in New Mexico

WALTER SCHMID

Translated by RICHARD RUNDELL
Edited by WOLFGANG T. SCHLAUCH

University of New Mexico Press
Albuquerque

Published in cooperation with the
Historical Society of New Mexico

10 09 08 07 06 05   1 2 3 4 5 6

Library of Congress Cataloging-in-Publication Data

Schmid, Walter, 1922–
  A German POW in New Mexico / Walter Schmid ; translated into English
by Richard Rundell ; with chapter introductions by Wolfgang T. Schlauch.
      p. cm.
  Translated from German.
  "Published in cooperation with the Historical Society of New Mexico."
  Includes bibliographical references.
  ISBN 0-8263-3355-9 (cloth : alk. paper)
  1. Schmid, Walter, 1922– 2. World War, 1939–1945—Prisoners and prisons,
American. 3. World War, 1939–1945—Prisoners and prisons, British. 4. World
War, 1939–1945—Conscript labor—New Mexico. 5. World War, 1939–1945—
Personal narratives, German. 6. Prisoners of war—Germany—Biography. 7.
Prisoners of war—New Mexico—Las Cruces—Biography. 8. Prisoners of
war—Great Britain—Biography. 9. World War, 1939–1945—Campaigns—
Africa, North. I. Title: German prisoner of war in New Mexico. II. Title.
  D805.5.L37S36 2005
  940.54'7273'092—dc22

                                    2004028009

Publication of this book has been supported in part by a generous grant from
the Historical Society of New Mexico.

Book design and composition by Damien Shay
Body type is Bembo 10.5/14 • Display is Papyrus and Impact

Contents

Introduction

by Wolfgang T. Schlauch

Walter Schmid, born and raised in a small town near Stuttgart, Germany, was twenty years old when he was drafted into the German army in 1942. After completion of his basic training, Walter's unit was shipped to Tunisia, Africa, at the end of December 1942 at a time when the German *Afrika Korps* under Field Marshal Erwin Rommel was already in the process of retreating. At the beginning of January 1943, Walter and his unit experienced their first battle against British and French forces. Later, as a machine gunner and frequent participant in reconnaissance patrols, he was exposed to risky battlefield operations. Slightly wounded, Walter witnessed the *Afrika Korps's* rapid collapse. On May 13, 1943, a quarter of a million German and Italian forces capitulated to the Allies.

Having experienced actual combat in North Africa for only five months, Walter surrendered to the British in Tunisia, who transferred him and many of the captured prisoners of war (POWs) to an American POW camp near Algiers, Algeria. Together with three hundred German POWs, Walter was shipped from the port of Oran to New York in June 1943 and from there to Camp Gruber in Oklahoma.

Walter was one of eventually 11 million German soldiers captured by the Allies during World War II. Of those, almost 380,000 were interned in the United States. During the latter part of the war, the United States captured an additional 3.4 million Germans in Europe who were held in captivity in France, Italy, and Germany, many of whom the U.S. Army would release in the summer of 1945, only a few months after the end of the war. Altogether, the United States held 436,788 prisoners of war on its soil: 378,898 Germans, 52,455 Italians, and 5,435 Japanese.

Members of the *Afrika Korps,* to which Walter belonged, regarded themselves as an elite fighting force who felt superior not only to some of their captors, but also to those fellow German POWs who were later captured in the Italian campaigns and during and after the Normandy invasion. They were taken prisoner at a time when the German *Wehrmacht* still occupied large parts of Europe. Many POWs from the *Afrika Korps* were hardened battlefield veterans who believed in Nazi Germany's final victory even after the Normandy invasion.

Walter, unlike many of his comrades who had been fighting in Africa since the beginning of the Africa campaign in 1941, had been in combat for only five months. He realized that the *Afrika Korps* had lost the battle in Africa to an overpowering Allied force. Massive quantities of Allied war materiel, which he saw during his train transfer from Tunisia to Algeria, made Walter think about the possible outcome of the war. At the time, he felt sorry for Germany and pondered what would happen if all this military hardware were to be used against his country.

Walter's first POW camp in the United States was Camp Gruber, a large base camp located in Oklahoma that could hold approximately five thousand prisoners. After a few weeks of inactivity, Walter was called upon to work first in a quarry and then mostly in agriculture. In addition to Camp Gruber, he stayed in a small branch facility, Camp Bixby, and finally in Camp McAlester, both located in Oklahoma, before being transferred to New Mexico.

The Geneva Convention of 1929, which had been signed by the United States and Germany, has numerous provisions concerning the treatment of POWs. Article twenty-seven specifically permits countries at war to employ POWs as laborers if they are physically fit, excluding officers and persons of equivalent status. It stipulates, however, that the workload of the POWs should not exceed that of civilian workers. Moreover, it prohibits the employment of POWs in military-related industries and the transport of military materiel destined for combat units.

Introduction

This provision of the Geneva Convention proved to be of particular importance for the United States. Only a few months after the United States entered World War II, it became obvious that the nation faced a major manpower shortage. Foreign workers could fill jobs formerly occupied by men who had been drafted only to a limited extent. One way to lessen the manpower deficiency was to utilize Italian and German POWs who were being shipped to the United States by the thousands after their capture in North Africa in the spring of 1943.

Initially, POW labor was used at military installations where the prisoners performed menial work so that American personnel could be transferred to combat duty. It soon became evident, however, that POW labor was also urgently needed in the private sector, particularly in agriculture.

In May 1942, the United States held only thirty-two Axis prisoners, but by April 1943, that number had increased to five thousand, including a small number of Japanese. By June 1943, one month after the defeat of the *Afrika Korps,* the U.S. accepted 53,435. In December 1943, the number of POWs in the United States swelled to 172,879. After the Normandy invasion and the Allied offensive across France, the United States held 360,000 POWs. By 1945, the number of Axis POWs still located in the United States was 4221,130.

Where were all those prisoners to be housed? In addition to placing POWs in unused military bases, the American government converted numerous abandoned Civilian Conservation Corps (CCC) camps into prisoner-of-war internment camps. By March 1943, the War Department had 37 camps set up on or near military installations. By August 1943, seventy-two camps had been established, and in April 1945, 500 prisoner-of-war camps were scattered through the United States. In addition to about 150 base camps, some of which could house up to 5,000 prisoners, the War Department established close to 350 branch or side camps. These could accommodate between 200 and 250 POWs and were usually located in areas where the prisoners were desperately needed as a labor force, mostly in rural areas.

Various government agencies and the War Department reached an agreement in 1943, on the basis of which civilian employers, farmers included, could officially request POWs to work for them. This outside work became known as "contract labor." Farmers and other employers could submit requests for POW labor to local authorities at a time when an increasing number of Americans were being drafted into the armed forces. The Army stipulated, however, that POW labor could only be hired out as contract labor if civilian labor was nonexistent in the area. Moreover, employers had to pay an hourly wage that was equivalent to the prevailing wage scale for civilian or "free" labor in that area.

The individual prisoner of war received eighty cents in canteen coupons for a full day's work. The employer had to pay the difference between what the prisoner received and the daily wages of a "free" worker to the U.S. Treasury, which in turn used the earnings to defray costs for maintaining and guarding POWs. By June 1945, employers who had contracted POW labor had paid twenty million dollars to the federal government.

The War Department, in addition to the Departments of Justice and State and other U.S. government agencies, wanted to make sure that the Army strictly applied provisions of the 1929 Geneva Convention to the POWs held in the United States. It regarded the Geneva Convention as a "treaty entered by this government," which is "bound to its terms and spirit." Article two of the Convention specifically stipulates that prisoners of war shall be treated humanely and are protected against violence and reprisals. In case of the violation of these rights, the POWs, based on Article forty-two, have the privilege to submit complaints to representatives of their "protecting power."

With the beginning of hostilities between Nazi Germany and the United States in December 1941, Switzerland became the "protecting power" of German POWs in the U.S. In addition, international organizations, such as the International Committee of the Red Cross (ICRC) and the YMCA (Young Men's Christian Association) cared for the welfare of the POWs and had the right to inspect POW camps and represent the internees' interests. Usually, a delegate from the U.S. State Department accompanied representatives of the Swiss legation, the ICRC, or the YMCA. Complaints by POWs or their designated spokesman were reported through the representatives of these organizations to the German Foreign Office, the State Department and eventually to the War Department. The ICRC visited Walter Schmid's POW branch camp in Las Cruces, New Mexico, twice.

Historians generally agree that POW labor proved to be enormously useful to the American war effort. During 1944 and 1945, Italian and German prisoners of war produced more than 1.2 billion man-hours of

Introduction

paid work in army installations, POW camps, and in contract employment. From 1943 to the end of December 1945, POWs generated more than thirty-four million man-days of contract labor, of which almost twenty-one million days were executed on farms. Based on an analysis of POW labor published by the Department of the Army, the employment of prisoners of war was essential to the welfare and economy of the United States. The study reaches the following conclusion: "Crops vital to the economy of our nation were harvested that otherwise would have been spoiled, and war industries were able to continue operations in the face of civilian manpower shortage. Both civil and military authorities have stated that they could not have performed their functions except for the use of prisoner of war labor."[*]

Walter was one of many who contributed to the American war effort. After a brief stint at Camp McAlester, Oklahoma, Walter and 340 other POWs were transferred to Las Cruces, New Mexico, at the end of July 1944. Since the military draft and the attraction of urban industrial jobs had drained the labor market, Mesilla Valley farmers, like farmers throughout the state of New Mexico and the entire country, were desperate for farm labor.

After almost three years of captivity, Walter and his fellow POWs were anxious to be repatriated. It came, however, as a great shock to them when, after their arrival in Europe, they learned that their captivity was to be extended in order to assist in the reconstruction of countries that had been devastated by the Germans during the war. Instead of being released to Germany, Walter was transferred to England, where he had to work for another year.

Finally, after more than four years of captivity, Walter was released in July 1947. Despite his criticism of some aspects of his imprisonment, Walter has revisited some of the places in England where he worked as a POW. He has returned to Las Cruces four times already, the last time in the spring of 2002, shortly after his eightieth birthday. There, he met his former Mexican-American friends with whom he had worked in the Mesilla Valley fields. He has also given interviews to news reporters

---

[*] George Lewis and John Mewha, *History of Prisoner of War Utilization by the United States Army: 1776–1945* (Washington, D.C.: Department of the Army, 1955), 265.

and historians at the New Mexico Farm and Ranch Heritage Museum about his experience as a POW.

Walter Schmid's memoir provides a vivid insight of an odyssey many soldiers on both sides experienced during World War II: battleground experience, captivity, long separation from family and home, loneliness, isolation, and the uncertainty of the future. Walter's narrative exposes the frailty of human nature under stress. It also demonstrates the impact ideological indoctrination can have on individuals.

The original version of Walter Schmid's book was published in Germany in 2000. It is considerably longer and contains a chapter describing his battlefield experience in North Africa. The abbreviated English translation is divided into four major chapters. The first chapter focuses on Walter's capture in North Africa and his voyage to the United States. Chapters two and three center on his experience as a prisoner of war in Oklahoma and New Mexico. The fourth chapter concentrates on his stay and work experience in England and his return to Germany.

The appendix includes Walter's meticulously kept diary from the period when he was a POW in Las Cruces, two poems he wrote in Las Cruces, International Red Cross reports from the Las Cruces POW camp, pay records issued by the U.S. Army, censored letters to his girlfriend in Germany, and a letter from British Labour Party Councillor H. Handford. The two poems Walter wrote during his captivity in Las Cruces reflect his amazement at the barren Organ Mountains, the scorching sun and the desert, the life-giving river, and the "happy people" living in the fertile valley.

Walter Schmid's memoir will be of interest to the general public and particularly to the people of Oklahoma and New Mexico. His book is also ideally suited for the classroom, predominantly for such courses that focus on World War II, "history and memory," or center on the subject of civil liberties and the 1929 Geneva Convention.

On a personal note, I would like to mention that I thoroughly enjoyed interviewing Walter Schmid both in Germany and Las Cruces for many hours about his experience as a prisoner of war. Walter at age eighty-three is physically fit and mentally alert.

A word of caution is in order that Walter's memoir might contain information based on rumors and hearsay, common in POW camps, rather than on hard facts. Also, after a hiatus of more than fifty years, some of

Introduction

the details he mentions might have been blurred by time or affected by long-held preconceptions. Yet Walter can vividly recall his experience picking cotton or harvesting cantaloupes in the Mesilla Valley, making friends with young Mexican-Americans in the fields, playing trumpet in the camp orchestra, or watching soccer games on Sundays between the teams of the two POW camps. Most of all, during his four years of captivity, he remembers his yearning to return to his little town in Germany to start a new life after a devastating war.

CHAPTER ONE

Capture and Voyage to America, 1943

INTRODUCTION

*I*n his first chapter, Walter Schmid describes his surrender to the British forces in Tunisia on May 11, 1943, only two days before the final capitulation of the Afrika Korps. Despite his realization that almost all of "our ships were sunk, and our air force was out of action," and his observation that the Allies had available an "almost unimaginable amount" of war materiel, Walter, like many of his comrades, still seemed to believe in the "final victory" of Nazi Germany. In fact, he did not anticipate being a POW for almost four and a half years. Imprisonment, he believed, would only be brief, as Germany would soon win the war.

How could he and his comrades have deluded themselves so completely? Until the capitulation of the German Sixth Army in Stalingrad in February 1943 and the Afrika Korps in North Africa in the spring of the same year, the German armies had been victorious and had occupied large parts of Europe. Having been indoctrinated with Nazi ideology, the belief in the superiority of the German master race, and the invincibility of the German armies, many German soldiers in 1943 still believed in and hoped for a German victory,

1

despite the devastating defeats on the eastern front and in Africa. This was particularly the case with the men of the Afrika Korps, *who did not foresee or want to acknowledge the possibility of the* Wehrmacht's *defeat and the collapse of Nazi Germany at the time of their capture. In contrast to German soldiers who were captured later in the Italian campaign, and particularly during and after the Normandy invasion, many soldiers of the* Afrika Korps *maintained their loyalty to Adolf Hitler.*

Walter, though not a hard-core adherent of Nazi ideology, had been exposed to Nazi propaganda. After having gone through the normal registration procedures in the American POW camp in Algeria, he felt that he had "almost no rights left." He bemoaned the fact that "any Negro could kick us in the ass," which "was a painful experience for us German soldiers, who allegedly belonged to the Master Race." Also, when he and his fellow prisoners encountered American soldiers who spoke German and who attempted to converse with them, they thought that these were German Jews. Walter emphatically states that the POWs did not want to have anything to do with them.

Many POWs had the mistaken notion that most German-speaking Americans were Jews who had escaped from Nazi Germany and who now served in the U.S. Army as interpreters, doctors, or guards. The POWs expected these individuals to take revenge on the POWs for what the Nazis had done to the Jews in Germany. Walter discovered, however, that German-speaking Jews treated the internees in a fair and just manner.

Walter's voyage together with three hundred fellow POWs from Oran, Algeria, across the Mediterranean and Atlantic to New York, on the American troop carrier Indiana, *was rather uneventful with the exception of the explosion of depth charges. In 1943, German submarines continued to attack Allied convoys, but none of the troop transports carrying POWs was sunk.*

Unlike most German POWs, crammed uncomfortably in the hold of their troop carrier and experiencing severe seasickness, Walter seems to have enjoyed his Atlantic crossing. He was surprised when one day a black guard secretly handed him a package, which contained a whole roast chicken, still warm, a Hershey's chocolate bar, and two oranges. This incident must have changed Walter's perception of American blacks.

Walter's impression of America was overwhelming. Besides passing the imposing Statue of Liberty in New York harbor, Walter was amazed at seeing New York City brightly lit at night and "neon advertising signs blinking on the skyscrapers." Also, the "loud traffic" in New York's streets on a Sunday evening surprised him. Walter, like all Germans, had been used to a total blackout of German cities since the beginning of World War II, a measure imposed by the Nazi regime to prevent enemy planes from locating their targets. Also, German civilian traffic had been drastically reduced due to the severe rationing of fuel.

Walter was one of many German POWs who had believed in widely spread rumors that suggested that the German Luftwaffe had bombed major American cities and inflicted heavy damage on American industrial centers. He and most of his comrades were certainly taken aback to see American cities, industries, and the countryside fully intact, and ports and railroad centers bustling with traffic.

Another shock waiting for Walter and his fellow POWs was the comfortable and upholstered Pullman cars the prisoners boarded in New York. Moreover, they could hardly believe that black waiters would serve the prisoners meals on trays. Most German soldiers had been used to being transported in boxcars throughout Germany and Europe and certainly without being waited on.

After an exciting sixty-five-hour train ride through the diverse American countryside and through cities such as Philadelphia, Cincinnati, St. Louis, and Kansas City, the German prisoners arrived at Camp Gruber, Oklahoma. Life in a POW camp in the United States began for Walter.

— WOLFGANG T. SCHLAUCH

I wrote this report in 1996 based on my diaries and from memory. Although it was not written for a museum in America, nonetheless, I am pleased that the New Mexico Farm and Ranch Heritage Museum in Las Cruces is interested in my memoirs. Keep in mind that I wrote this account as I experienced it at the time. The stories that I wrote about the young Mexican-Americans, particularly Junior Barela, they confirmed for me during a September 1998 visit. My sincere thanks to Mr. Bob Hart for his friendly and instructive tour of the museum. I wish him, his colleagues, and the museum the best of luck in the future.

MY ROAD TO AFRICA

I was born on 19 March 1922 in Gross-Sachsenheim, Germany, not far from Stuttgart. When the war began in September 1939, I was only seventeen

3

years old and confident that I would not have to participate in it. It was supposed to be a short war, and victory would not take long. Unfortunately, things turned out differently. My age group 1922 was called upon on 19 December [1939] in Bietigheim, but I was not actually drafted into the army until 17 April 1942, because I was employed in tool making at Kienle and Spiess, a firm considered vital to the war effort. I was drafted into a signals company in the grenadiers' base in Zuffenhausen, as a radioman and telephonist. After ten days in the barracks, I came down with scarlet fever, which delayed my basic training. But by 29 September [1942], I was ready to move out with my unit via France, Germany, Austria, Yugoslavia, Greece, and Italy to North Africa. We arrived in Tunis on 22 December 1942 and were shipped directly to the front.

The German *Afrika Korps* under General Rommel was in retreat from Libya to Tunisia. Those of us who had been shipped directly to Tunisia were meant to relieve the weakened forces and stop the pursuing British. Initially, we were successful at this, but then the Americans landed in Casablanca, Morocco, with enormous materiel support. They advanced toward Tunisia from the west, whereas we were hardly receiving supplies. Almost all of our ships were sunk, and our air force was out of action. It became impossible for us to continue fighting. On 13 May 1943, the uneven battle was ended when the *Afrika Korps* surrendered.

I had been wounded in the leg shortly before the end, so I did not see action in the final battle but was in the supply unit. Together with a wounded Italian soldier, I moved into the mountains on the Cap Bon peninsula in the hope of escaping somehow, but in vain.

Near me was a German resupply unit with ten brand-new Mercedes trucks, which were not going to be used and were simply waiting for the end. We attached ourselves to this unit, since they still had enough provisions.

On 11 May, we could hear only isolated artillery fire. Enemy aircraft were still in the air but were no longer attacking. The naval artillery on the warships in the Gulf of Tunis was quiet. Suddenly there was an eerie silence.

We were nervous about what would happen then. We saw an English tank approaching in a dust cloud and realized that this was it. An officer of the resupply unit got in his VW jeep, tied a white rag to the antenna, and took off toward the tank.

Both vehicles met, an English officer got out, and both officers approached each other and saluted, then shook hands. They talked for quite a while. We were anxious about the outcome. They shook hands once more, saluted, got back into their respective vehicles, and turned around. We were eager to hear the report. "Listen up," said our officer, "I have just surrendered us to the English. We are now to be considered prisoners of war. No one is allowed to keep a weapon, and there must be no more hostile action. The English have advised us to stay here tonight, to get a good night's sleep, and head for Tunis in the morning." After he had given us this news, he went to the Italians and repeated it.

My Italian friend left me and went back to his comrades. What we still had left by way of weaponry, we threw into the sea. I had actually wanted to take my Luger pistol home with me. After a quiet night, the first without the noise of war, everyone had a bath and a shave and was in good spirits. After a hearty breakfast, the remaining provisions were divided up. We then set out for our journey into imprisonment in two old trucks. We had been observing the Italians to see what they would do. They realized that they had no more vehicles left, since everything had been destroyed. They dashed over to us, wringing their hands, and begged us to take them along. But we were already packed together standing in the back of the truck. They climbed onto the running boards, sat on the hood, and held on wherever they could. Thus we set out like a cluster of human grapes. We didn't get rid of them until Tunis.

The morning of 13 May was sunny. Peace was evident everywhere, and we calmly approached our fate. When we reached the main highway, we saw a horrible sight. On either side of the road, as far as the eye could see, there were still burning vehicles, as well as many half-burnt and deformed corpses, some of them still hanging out of the vehicles. Dead pack mules and camels lay with their legs sticking out, their bellies swollen to bursting. A revoltingly sweet smell was everywhere; here the final battle had taken place. The heat lay over this field of death like a shroud. Only a small pathway had been cleared, and we drove slowly and soberly through this battlefield. How could human beings do this to other human beings, all of us Christians, with the same Bible? We all believed in the same merciful God, but where was He now?

We left the peninsula for a short trip to Tunis, wondering what awaited us there. More and more trucks were on the road, moving in both directions, and soon we were part of an endless column. Individual English and American soldiers stood on the side of the road waving the vehicles on.

Tunis came into view, and we entered the city, with Arabs waving to us enthusiastically, as if we were the victors. Our enemies simply smiled. The column ground to a halt. Arabs tried to sell us everything imaginable. I had saved three thousand Tunisian francs to buy a carpet, but now I didn't know what to do with the money. From one Arab I bought a bag of sweetened pastry for fifty francs, an outrageous price, but what did it matter now?

Barely moving, we drove through the city, passing familiar streets and squares, always through files of waving Arabs. After we had left Tunis, we were stopped. A German-speaking Englishman told us that we were no longer permitted to leave the highway. Anyone seen away from the highway could be shot.

We drove south from Tunis to Mejez el Bab. The column had thinned out. Other vehicles had apparently been sent in different directions. After almost two hours in the blazing hot sun, we discovered a large accumulation of people. As we approached, we saw that it was a prisoner-of-war camp, filled with soldiers. We drove up to the gate and were met by English military police who told us to drive on, since this camp was already full. By then, it was late afternoon, and we needed to find a camp by nightfall.

We drove on in this bizarre situation, German soldiers searching for their own prison camp. We saw a large area surrounded by barbed wire and thinking this might be a camp, we drove up to it. Yes, we could stay here. Our driver poured sugar into the tank to ruin the engine. We didn't want to leave the enemy with a usable vehicle.

PRISONER OF WAR

We took our symbolic steps through the camp gate from freedom into confinement, although I had already given up most of my own freedom when I had entered the barracks as a draftee. But this was worse. I was a prisoner of war for four and a half years. Luckily, none of us suspected it would be that long. Imprisonment could only be brief, because soon Germany would have won the war. How one can delude oneself!

Once again, I was one of many. 130,000 German soldiers were taken prisoner in North Africa, with 18,000 dead and 3,400 missing in action. In little Tunisia alone, there were 8,560 dead and 3,400 missing. All of those who died in Tunisia are in the German military cemetery Bord Jedria twelve miles south of Tunis. This military cemetery is located on a well-tended hill.

THE FIRST CAMP

The British camp was a huge sandpit with a few poplar trees. There was barbed wire all around the camp, with a wide path through the middle. On each side were enclosures with normal wire for one hundred men each, packed in snugly. But one could walk all around the camp at leisure. There was no checkpoint at the gate and no search for weapons. Because it had just been opened up, it was still fairly empty. Right at the entrance, I was put in the second unit of one hundred. Others were brought in continually, so the camp filled up quickly. Most of them came in groups, some in complete companies. Only I was by myself.

Another man was also by himself, and we got together, which made things easier. Each of us could look around the camp for a while, searching for friends, while the other looked after his things. The few belongings each of us still had, we didn't want stolen. Emil Gröschl from Graz, Austria, had just turned twenty-one, as had I, and was by trade a waiter in a hotel in Graz. We stayed together all the way to New York.

The first few days, we had nothing at all to eat. Only the water truck came every day. There was always a frightful crowding then, and half of the water was lost. Since it stopped right at the entrance, those of us up front had the best chance. Nor was there any medical attention yet, and my wound could not be tended to. At the edge of the camp was a small brook, but now, in May, it was merely a trickle. Many men washed their bandages in it, or at least their feet. I didn't risk washing myself there, and I left the bandage on my leg as it was.

After a few days, the first provisions arrived. The British threw a few packages of cookies into each group of one hundred. The highest-ranking man had to count them first, then figure out how many each man would get. Usually there was only half a cookie per man per day. Even the crumbs had to be divided up, and everyone made sure it was done fairly. We would have starved if almost every one of us had not had some food with him, but this quickly ran out.

The mood of the camp was bad. We lay close to each other on the bare ground. During the day, the sun shone down relentlessly, and we had no shade. At night, it grew uncomfortably cold. We kept getting up to walk around and warm up. In this way we waited for the days to pass. Luckily, it was always fair weather; who knows what would have happened if it had rained.

In the crowded camp, I caught sight of our driver, Scheele. He was here together with our sergeant and the office staff. He thought I should move over to them, in the back of the camp. Above all, I should go to the sergeant, who would promote each of us, since he had official rubber stamps and all the forms. Thus I could become a non-commissioned officer on the spot. I thanked him but said no. If I hadn't deserved a promotion under normal circumstances, I didn't want one now, nor did I want to move back with them. I didn't want to see any of them, I was so angry with the company leadership.

After four days in the camp, there was some unrest, and the British guards came running. The first groups of one hundred had to line up in rows of five. We left the camp, marched several miles along the road, and came to a train station. There stood a long freight train with closed boxcars. Forty men in every car, each much smaller than those of a German train. After the entire column had been loaded, the train jolted forward and headed west on a single spur. We all wondered where we were going and how long the trip would be. There was room enough to stand, but it was impossible for everyone to lie down. It grew very hot in the boxcar, with nothing but small ventilation slits bringing some draft into the hot air. Night came, and the train kept going. We got tired standing and discussed what to do. We couldn't all lie down at once, even on our sides like sardines; some of us would have to stand. So we took turns sleeping. We were lying so tightly packed that we all had to turn over at the same time. I was having trouble with my wounded leg. I kept getting kicked by my neighbor, which caused me great pain every time.

None of us knew where we were going or how long the trip would be. The doors were locked from the outside. The guards, who were French, rode on top of the boxcars armed with rifles. The next morning, the train stopped on the open line, and the doors were opened. Finally we could get out and walk around in the open, but only on one side of the train. That was a relief. Then we got a thin soup, a piece of bread, and a cupful of water in each canteen, and that was all until the next day.

We climbed back aboard, the doors were locked again, and the journey continued. The cars rocked back and forth on the worn tracks so that we almost grew seasick. We could see out only through the ventilation slits. The landscape grew more and more deserted, nothing but sand and bare mountains. But then we saw something that gave us pause. To the left and right of the train tracks, we saw gigantic piles, each as tall as a man, of American bombs, shells, crates of ammunition, going on for kilometers. It was an almost unimaginable amount; then came airfields with runways covered with perforated steel panels, and aircraft as far as the eye could see. Then came long columns of vehicles of every kind. For hours, we passed this abundance of materiel. Poor Germany, if all this materiel were used against us.

On a train station sign, we could just make out the place name "Constantine," so we were now in Algeria. Every evening, the doors were again opened, out on the open line, but only long enough to stretch our legs.

We had an older, gray-haired man in our boxcar who got diarrhea, which created a new problem; he groaned as he tossed and turned. He couldn't hold it in and defecated in his pants. After a while, he started up again. We were sorry for him, but we couldn't do anything for him. Then someone suggested cutting a hole in one of the floor planks. Almost all of us had knives, so we went to work, motivated by the man's groans. After considerable labor, we had made a fist-sized hole, and that had to do. When he had to go again, two men held him over the hole, and he could empty his bowels, although some of the contents missed the hole. This had to be scraped into the hole with a knife blade; it wasn't a very pleasant job.

The whole boxcar stank dreadfully, and we could hardly stand it. But what choice did we have? The man apologized again and again, but that didn't make the stench subside. He couldn't help it. So we gradually got used to the routine of the trip. Four young men from Vienna offered some variety by singing old Viennese songs in harmony. We all enjoyed listening, but they didn't want to sing alone; they wanted us to join in. So we all learned Viennese songs, such as "Giddyup, Old Horse, Giddyup" ["Hüaho, alter Schimmel, Hüaho"]. With singing, the time passed more rapidly, and the old man got better, too. Still, it was hardly an enjoyable journey. By day, it was terribly hot in the boxcar, and at night, it grew bitterly cold; and we were always thirsty. The hunger wasn't so bad.

A few men still had their shelter-halves [tents] with them, since we had never been searched. These we attached somehow to the ceiling of the boxcar so that everyone could sleep at once. The old man had to sleep over the hole. But it was still so cramped that we could only turn over at the same time. We got used to this, too. We been under way for six days, with the soup growing more and more watery and no bread left. Then we found out that the guards, when we stopped at train stations to wait for traffic bound in the other direction, were unloading crates of our rations to the Arabs.

A large city drew into view, and the train crossed numerous switch-points. This could only be Algiers. At the station, our train stopped. We were soon surrounded by young people; apparently trains like ours were arriving every day. They yelled at us, threw rocks at the ventilation slits, and climbed up on the boxcars to stick poles and bars inside. We had to crouch down as it got more and more dangerous; they were behaving wildly. One of them climbed up onto our car and held fast to the ventilation slit with his fingers. One of us took a shoe and pounded its heel on the man's fingers with all his strength. He fell with a cry of pain. Now we were afraid they would take revenge, but at that moment, the train started up again.

After Algiers, we noticed that the train was again headed south. Then, on the seventh day, the trip was over, when we arrived in Sidi-Bel-Abbés in Algeria. This city was famous as the headquarters of the French Foreign Legion. Their training camp was here on the edge of the desert. From the train station, we marched in a long column past their barracks to a prisoner-of-war camp well outside of the French base, run by the American army.

This was a gigantic camp with high barbed-wire fences, with large tents for the guards and for the kitchens. Right at the entrance, a long row of tables had been set up, with American soldiers behind them. Every one of us had to go to one of the tables, strip naked, and lay all his clothes and belongings on the table. Then we went, with only our wallets, to the next row of tables. Each of us was examined, the personal data from his ID papers recorded, and we were fingerprinted. All money was confiscated, placed in envelopes, and labeled with the man's name, then back we went to the first tables. In the meantime, everything had been sorted out, and almost all of it confiscated.

Now we learned what it meant to be a prisoner of war. We had almost no rights left. Any Negro could kick us in the ass. This was a painful experience for us German soldiers, who allegedly belonged to the Master Race. But we still believed in a German victory, and then we'd pay them back. It was clear, we had to win this war, if Germany were not to be destroyed.

Only a tiny pile remained; everything was gone except for basic items of clothing and papers. It had all been tossed onto a heap behind the table: mirrors, mess kits, canteens, scissors—everything went into the heap. Since Gröschl and I weren't first in line, and managed to see what was going on,

Capture and Voyage to America, 1943

I first threw away the letters that I had found on the dead British soldiers. I didn't want to be held responsible for the massacre of the fleeing British troops. We had no idea what the victors were going to do with us. Other comrades even still had food with them, which they had carefully hoarded. They stuffed themselves with whatever they had. Things were being thrown away left and right, as one could see on the ground. For fun, I stuck my pocket mirror and fingernail scissors into Gröschl's cap, when he bent over in front of me. He didn't even notice it.

Now it was my turn. I had to strip, lay everything on the table, and move on to the next table. A man who must have been a physician looked me over from head to foot and asked me in German why my leg was bandaged. He didn't want to see the wound, but only my paybook, from which he recorded the data (the page pertaining to my unit I had already torn out, as had the other soldiers).

My 2,950 francs he stuck in a large envelope with my name and a registration number, then he took my fingerprints and sent me back to the first table. All that lay there were my clothes, shoes, shaving gear, my English dictionary, and a piece of soap; I got dressed again.

After everyone had been thus processed, which took several hours, we were distributed throughout the camp. We had to form up in groups of four, which then got assigned a tent. These were quite low tents, double-length, two men on each side, heads together in the middle, with thin straw mattresses on the sand. I moved into our tent with Emil Gröschl, Adolf Hohl from Reutlingen, and Bernhardt Feldhaus. It was cramped, but we were all right.

No one had anything left to eat; now we were all equally hungry. After hours of waiting, until everyone had been assigned quarters, there was a meal. We lined up, each with a tray, and moved past a food distribution point where everyone got a ladle-full of food. It looked tasty and tasted good, but there was too little of it for our hungry bellies. For drinking water, there were a number of large canvas containers of ice water at various points throughout the camp. We could help ourselves from several small faucets, using paper cups, which were provided. We weren't used to anything like this. It was a marvelous set-up, to be able to drink ice water whenever we wanted. We were able to wash at long troughs, which always had enough water. From time to time, showers were also turned on, which were especially welcome.

For the first time in weeks, I took off my bandage. The wound didn't look good. A scab was forming, but it wasn't draining any more. I could now finally wash my bandage.

The Cancie camp in Algeria lay at the edge of the desert. During the day, we couldn't stand the heat inside our tents. But there were large open-sided tents in the middle of the camp where the air could move through. Sandstorms kept coming from the desert with gusts of wind. Then we all had to stay in our tents and hold them down so they wouldn't be blown away. The sand came through every crack, and we could constantly taste it in our mouths, but otherwise life in the camp was bearable. By now, we didn't expect much. The latrine was in a corner of the camp, primitive wooden seats over an open ditch. When the wind blew from that direction, the stench spread over the entire camp.

After several days, it occurred to me that Gröschl still had my mirror and nail scissors in his cap. He was amazed to learn about them. They were still there, even though he wore his cap all day. We were glad to have these items and were the only ones who had such things.

Preprinted postcards were distributed for us to write to our families in Germany, only a brief greeting and word that we were all right. These cards made it back to Germany, too. Everyone in the *Afrika Korps* had been reported at home as missing in action.

In the evenings, when it got cool, comrades with various performing talents displayed them in an open area in the camp. One Swabian comic in particular entertained us delightfully.

American soldiers who spoke German kept walking around between the tents and trying to start conversations with us. We heard they were German Jews, and we wanted nothing to do with them.

Outside of the camp, the French Foreign Legionnaires wearing their white caps marched to their drill areas in the desert. Each evening, they came back exhausted and drenched in sweat; we were better off.

Until Sunday, 3 June [1943], I was in this camp. That morning, we assembled and marched through Sidi-Bel-Abbés to the station. On the way, we encountered a group of children all dressed up, the girls in white dresses with flowers in their hair, the boys in black suits and bow ties, all holding candles. It was apparently the Catholics'"White Sunday." The contrast could not have been more striking: here a column of defeated, lice-infected prisoners (we still had lice), and there happy children going to church with their parents. It seemed like a fairy tale to us that such things could still be taking place.

At the train station stood a long freight train with open cars, into each of which fifty men were stuffed, standing like sardines. The sun burning down on us was made bearable only by the wind of the moving train. We were headed north, and standing got more and more uncomfortable. After four hours' journey, we approached a large city and even saw the sea in the distance. That had to be Oran, Algeria, which we were nearing from the heights; its port lay beneath us. In long switchbacks, the train slowly descended. Then we saw some people on the raised embankment, apparently waiting for us. That seemed nice of them. But we soon learned differently; they were waiting for us with rocks, empty bottles, and wooden sticks. A hailstorm of objects was thrown at us, and we couldn't protect ourselves. Everyone tried to duck, but when many of us were hit, a triumphal cry arose. We threw back some of the rocks we were able to catch, but a number of us were hurt.

THE PORT OF ORAN

Finally we entered the restricted harbor and were safe from the mob outside. In the harbor were many ships, most of them American freighters, some rusty, some new. Which one would be ours? We marched past one after another, but only one was tied up at the pier, and that one was ours. We climbed aboard by a simple gangway; we didn't have any luggage. Only three hundred men came aboard the ship, the *Indiana,* an ex-German ship of ten thousand tons. After World War I, it had been taken by the French and now was in American service. The captain was French, but the crew was American.

We were confined forward in the upper hold. It was a large, windowless room, more like a hall. Only through the large open loading hatch above did fresh air and some light enter. There was no artificial lighting. We had to climb down by an iron ladder. There was room enough in the hold to spread out, but no bedding, just one life jacket and one blanket per man. We lay on the bare steel deck. Everyone found himself a place; Gröschl and I were neighbors. An airy latrine was on board, a simple wooden construction built up high above the railing. One had to climb up to it. Excrement fell directly into the ocean, a perfect disposal system.

THE VOYAGE

When all three hundred of us were on board, the ship cast off and sailed into the open sea, where it stopped and anchored. More and more ships collected in the following days, anchored in front of the port as far as the eye could see. Then, on the third day, we started to form into a convoy, and the journey began. On the next day, we passed Gibraltar, close to the African shore. For the last time for a long while to come, we looked upon Europe. A wooden keg of stagnant water was in our hold near the ladder. Everyone got a quart a day and could use it as he wished, for washing, shaving, or drinking.

Food on board consisted mainly of canned beans. There was no galley, but every few days we received an American one-man ration like American soldiers got at the front. This contained everything a man needed for a day: cigarettes, canned meat or sausage, bread, sugar, salt, bouillon cubes, even toilet paper, all of it packed in waterproof wrapping.

By day, we could go up on deck and had the forward section of the ship to ourselves. At night, only one man at a time could go up to use the latrine, with an armed guard patrolling. It was an experience for each of us to stand on deck at night and see the endless starry sky. Our ship was on the port outer flank of the convoy. As far as the eye could see, there were ships; we could count about eighty-five of them reaching to the horizon. Later, we learned from fellow POWs on other ships that only the outermost ships forward and aft, port, and starboard were laden with three hundred POWs each. The entire convoy had tankers in the middle but was listed with the International Red Cross as a POW convoy to protect it from German submarines. A few days later, we met another convoy headed eastward. The whole ocean was filled with ships of all sizes bearing war materiel to Europe, while ours returned empty.

It was never boring on deck. Off the bow there were flying fish, then there was only the wide, rolling sea and a sense of peace. No hectic activity any more, only the vibrations and pounding of the ship's engines. The hard floor didn't disturb our sleep; we were toughened by now. Our nerves, stressed for so long, calmed down. We were only worried about what would happen to us now.

Sometimes at night, it was a bit eerie, since the old ship creaked and groaned even in a mild sea, and the water slapped and splashed against the steel plating. We could imagine that steel plates only a fraction of an inch thick separated us from the depths of the sea. We sat or lay on deck with our shirts off. No one was worried about sunburn any more; all of us were well tanned. I actually enjoyed the ocean voyage. The sea was usually smooth as glass, without a cloud in the sky, with a pleasant breeze from our passage. The entire convoy traveled very slowly. One could have run just as fast, but since we kept going twenty-four hours a day, we made good distance.

We were sorry for the guards; surely we were no danger out here in mid-Atlantic. One night, with everyone below decks, we heard the sentries running excitedly on deck. Commands were given, and planks were placed over our loading hatch and covered with a tarpaulin. Now we were completely in darkness. This was strange and played havoc with our nerves, closed in at night. In an emergency, we would all drown miserably; not a one of us would get out.

Then we heard depth charges exploding nearby. But men who knew about such ordnance said they were far away. Still, we were scared. More and more depth charges were dropped, but they were now fading into the distance. We grew more hopeful, but no one was allowed up onto the latrine.

By our reckoning, it was morning when the cover was finally removed. Everyone breathed a sigh of relief and was able to go up on deck. The fresh air felt good, and the latrine brought relief. We looked around and saw that everything was as before, but then we noticed that one aircraft carrier was missing. Two aircraft carriers had been circling our convoy, and now one was absent; we never learned where it had gone.

There was also a shower on deck, with seawater pumped up to it. We sprayed each other with a large stream from a hose. But if we washed our hair with normal soap, it got completely gummed up. For salt water, one needed a special soap. Showering and washing went all right, but the salt water left a white crust on our bodies that burned unpleasantly for quite a while afterward. We had no fresh water for showering.

Again and again, the used toilet paper from our latrine floated on the breeze up to the bridge and stuck to the captain's windows. He didn't like that, of course, and gave an order to deposit the used paper in a bucket of water.

Our leisure area on deck was roped off, and American sentries with machine guns patrolled unhappily. They seemed intent upon not coming too near us. They wouldn't talk to us, although some of us spoke English.

I was therefore all the more surprised when a young, colored sentry with curly black hair kept walking back and forth near me. I was sitting near the rope and sensed that he wanted something from me. He kept glancing over at me unobtrusively. When he felt he was unobserved, he secretly gave me a sign to go below to our hold and wait aft. I couldn't imagine what that meant, and I hesitated, but he encouraged me to go. None of my comrades noticed anything.

To be on the safe side, I took Gröschl with me. He, too, wondered what was going on and found the matter strange. We climbed below and went aft. Just then, the hold was empty, since everyone was up on deck. We saw an opening in the ceiling through which one could look down into the hold. We sat down and waited, watching the opening nervously. Suddenly, a curly black head was visible, peeking down at us cautiously. When he saw a second man, he wanted to leave. I signaled to him that this was my friend. Then he showed the rest of himself, and we saw a small package in his hand. He wanted to know if the coast was clear, and we signaled yes. He lowered the package on a string. I opened it and found a whole roast chicken, still warm, with fresh rolls, a bar of Hershey's chocolate, and two oranges. This was quite a surprise.

I thanked him with gestures, and he disappeared smiling. We pounced on the food and ate everything, so that our comrades wouldn't notice anything. There was a smell of roast chicken in the air for a while, though. Why this soldier did that, and for me in particular, has remained a mystery to me to this day, but it pleased me enormously. I wanted to thank him somehow, but I didn't have a thing, and I couldn't shake his hand. It occurred to me that I still had some coins from Greece and Tunisia in my coin purse, and I wanted to give him those.

The next day, I sat in the same place while he was on duty. We winked at each other, then I unobtrusively lay the coins on the deck near my feet, close to the barrier. He watched me out of the corner of his eye. I stood up and moved away. He went over to the coins, bent over, and wiped off his shoe, then picked up the coins without drawing attention. He smiled as he looked over at me. No one else saw a thing.

On deck, I got a cinder in my eye that grew more and more painful, until after two days I could hardly stand it. I told one of the sentries. He immediately went up to the bridge and got two other sentries, who took me between them up to the bridge, keeping me covered with machine guns.

In a small cabin, I was told to lie down on a cot. A man in a white gown removed the cinder quickly and painlessly. The two sentries brought me back below, but at least I'd gotten to take a look at the bridge.

After twenty-four days on board, the crew was growing restless. Volunteers were requested, and many came forward, but not I. Under strict guard, they had to bring crates of provisions up and throw them overboard. This was incomprehensible to us. Some asked at least to be able to keep the cigarettes, but no, everything had to go overboard. A long trail of crates floated astern and disappeared in the distance. Such wastefulness was beyond our grasp—that was America. On the morning of 27 June, we saw what the crew had been looking for on the horizon. America couldn't be far away now, and we grew excited. What was waiting for us? In the distance, we saw a shadowy strip of coastline, and the soldiers started to cheer. We drew nearer to land, and soon we could see tall buildings. New York, here we come.

AMERICA, HERE WE ARE

Sunday evening, 27 June [1943], at eight o'clock, we sailed slowly past the famous Statue of Liberty. Everyone was on deck. No one wanted to miss this moment. Slowly we sailed on, until the ship came to a stop at one of the many piers. It had grown dark, and what a spectacle now greeted our eyes. Everything was lit up as brightly as day, with neon advertising signs blinking on the skyscrapers before us. There was an amazing amount of loud traffic in the streets on this Sunday evening. It was overwhelming to us, since we had been used to only darkness at night. None of us slept that night; we stayed on deck and enjoyed this unusual spectacle. We had to continue using our outboard latrine in port; some pedestrians may have wondered about this. That night, we had to stay on board the ship, and we didn't land the next morning either. A ferryboat picked us up, and after a brief trip, we stepped foot on American soil. No flags, no reception committee, no president to greet us.

From many reports and stories, we knew that German emigrants had come to America in the past. They sailed in cramped ships to Ellis Island. They were registered at the port, and their health was checked, and many of them were sent back. Not we—no passport check, no immigration permit, we simply disembarked onto land. We lined up and started marching between high buildings. Not a soul or vehicle was to be seen apart from our sentries; apparently everything had been roped off. We looked up at the high buildings, and one of the guards said in German, "Amazing, isn't it? I'll bet you don't have buildings like that in Germany." One man behind me said casually, "Are you kidding? Every chicken coop in Germany is that size." The guard was silent and looked insulted. All of the guards spoke German—you could almost think you were in a German city.

After a short march, we arrived at a giant hall, where clouds of steam covered everything. Right behind us was a column of Italian POWs, also about three hundred men, like ours. They went in front of us, which surprised us. But then it was our turn, and we had to strip naked, but we were used to it by now. Each of us got two string bags and an ID disk. All clothing went into one bag, while shoes, wallets, coin purses, papers, and anything else of leather went into the other bag.

We kept moving, to a long row of showers, which were producing all that steam, one man per showerhead. Hot water kept running continuously, and a bar of strong soap was in the holder. Here we could really have a thorough wash, which felt very good. We could get rid of our lice, too. We didn't want to leave the showers, but the next group was waiting. After the shower, we went down a narrow hall, and a Negro tossed each of us a fluffy white towel. We wanted to keep them after we'd dried off, but we had to throw them on a pile. On we went, past a long line of Negroes, each with a spray gun. They sprayed each of us with some strong liquid, especially wherever there was hair. Those with long hair got it cut with veterinary shears, which made them furious.

After this was a line of doctors. They examined every part of every one of us, to make sure all the lice were gone. They were, and we felt fresh as new. One doctor sent me to a bandaging station, where my bandage was removed and the wound examined. The doctor said I should be seen by another physician as soon as I reached camp. He put some salve on the wound and rebandaged it.

The whole procedure was now over, and all that was missing was our clothing. Gradually, all three hundred of us assembled again, all of us naked. It took almost an hour for baggage carts with our string bags to return. We all crowded around to find our own pairs of bags. The clothing was still warm. Not a single louse was to be found; they had been thorough. The other string bag had apparently been fumigated. But now a new problem developed. Our leather belts and suspenders had gotten subjected to so much heat that they were now cracked and falling apart. How were we going to keep our pants up? Everyone had his own solution. My pants stayed up, but I had to pull at them all the time.

When we were all ready, we formed up again and marched through empty streets to a train station. Apart from heavily armed soldiers, there were no civilians to be seen. We lined up in groups of ten on the station platform, with me standing next to Gröschl. Each group of ten marched off, then the next one, and the groups were broken up. Gröschl and I were separated; friends lost each other. Each group of ten joined another group of ten until all three hundred men had been assembled. These groups waited. Then the next unit of three hundred men arrived, and they were redistributed in the same way.

Each group was now a big mob. A suburban train arrived in a rush with screeching brakes. The first group got aboard quickly, the doors were closed, and the train departed. The next one arrived almost immediately. Now it was our group's turn, and the last of us was scarcely aboard before the train left. We raced through New York, sometimes underground, sometimes on elevated tracks, then at ground level again, with no stops, until we reached a suburban station.

We all got out and crossed several tracks to a waiting express train, where we were to embark. I was the first one on the platform and opened the door; it looked quite elegant, with padded seats. I started to close the door again quickly; this car couldn't possibly be for us, but a sentry urged me to get aboard. We moved with quiet reverence and found seats. One sentry who spoke German told us that three men should occupy four seats, leaving the fourth seat empty. This is the way we always traveled in America.

They were Pullman cars, but the windows were designed to be opened only a crack. At either end of each car were a toilet and a washroom, and in the aisle a water cooler on each side with ice water and paper cups. The seats were very comfortable. This would have been easy to take, if only we hadn't been so hungry. We hadn't had anything to eat since early morning on board ship, and now it was late in the evening.

The train traveled through the night, through the suburbs. A group of black men came through the car, each with a tray. The first one passed out plastic eating utensils, the second one plastic plates, and then came the food, also on trays. There was a variety, but too little of each thing. There was even a tiny dessert. We could get ice water to drink with permission from the sentry. This was the rule for going to the toilet, too.

Night fell, and we were tired after an eventful day. The clicking of the wheels put us to sleep. We dozed, but it was uncomfortable, trying to sleep sitting up, lying crookedly on the seats. Some of us just gave up and lay on the floor so they could stretch out. The floor soon grew crowded, too. The sentries hardly had room to stand. We pitied them having to stand guard in two-hour shifts at the door and keep an eye on us when we went to the toilet.

We were glad when it grew light. Now we could observe America in comfort. Large fields in a wide landscape, colorfully painted single-family houses everywhere. As we looked more closely, we could tell they were all wood houses. We saw men and women on their way to work. In the streets there was heavy traffic with large cars.

Breakfast arrived, as on the previous evening, on trays. Two pieces of toast, a spoonful of peanut butter—which was unfamiliar to us—a small serving of scrambled eggs, wrapped pats of butter, and a cup of tea or coffee, with an orange for dessert. After the meal, the plastic utensils and plates were simply thrown out of the narrowly opened windows onto the tracks, which looked cluttered. Our first big stop was at the Union Station in St. Louis. Roof tanks were filled with water. A work detail of black women thoroughly cleaned the cars inside and out.

One group came to our car, but when they saw the sentry with his machine gun and us, they were so frightened that they jumped out again with a cry. We laughed out loud. The sentry ran after them and talked to them on the platform for a while, calmed them down, and brought them back. But they only cleaned the toilet and the washroom, filled up the water coolers, and threw a few pieces of ice into them. They didn't come into the car where we sat and stood. Once they were outside again, they were clearly relieved.

By day, it was lovely to travel across America like this, with ever-changing landscapes. We didn't know where we were headed. We could vaguely sense the direction from the cities through which we passed: Philadelphia, Cincinnati, Kansas City—we must be headed toward the Southwest.

Finally, after a sixty-five-hour journey, we arrived on the morning of 1 July 1943 at Camp Gruber in Oklahoma. A short march to the camp, then a round-up. Everybody stripped, put their clothes on a big tarp, and stepped back. Everything was searched thoroughly. I was able to hide my nail scissors in the dirt under the tarp. My pocket mirror was confiscated. We got dressed again and formed a column. But I wanted those scissors. A guard standing next to me was waiting for me to get ready to move out. But I dawdled on purpose, and my comrades were getting impatient. Finally the sentry moved, I bent over and quickly retrieved my scissors, and joined the others. I still have those scissors today forty-five years later.

———

CHAPTER TWO

POW in Oklahoma, July 1943–July 1944

INTRODUCTION

*W*alter was pleasantly surprised when he arrived at Camp Gruber, Oklahoma, a large base camp that could house up to five thousand POWs. He found army cots, each with four blankets, a soft pillow, and toiletries on top of each bed. The food was excellent and plentiful, and Walter and his comrades felt that "they had landed in the right place."

Why did the United States provide the German POWs this unexpected lavish treatment? One of the major reasons for the U.S. government to treat these prisoners well was to induce the Nazi government to reciprocate. As tens of thousands of Americans were eventually taken prisoner by Nazi Germany, the U.S. government wanted to do everything possible to assure American captives in Germany decent treatment. Proper treatment of German POWs in the United States, the government hoped, would effect similar treatment of American prisoners in Nazi Germany. Though American POWs fared considerably worse than their German counterparts in the United States, Germany generally treated British and American POWs much better than prisoners of other nations. Germany, like the United States and Great Britain, was a signatory power of the Geneva Convention.

Walter, after several weeks of inactivity at Camp Gruber, was finally called to work, first in a quarry and then, in the fall of 1943, to harvest vegetables. According to the Geneva Convention, nations detaining enemy POWs were permitted to use them as labor as long as they were not employed in war-related industries and transportation. Initially, a POW could receive a maximum of 80¢ for a full day's work. In spring 1944, the Army introduced a pay plan on the basis of which a hardworking POW would earn a maximum of $1.20 per day. Instead of cash, the Army provided the POWs with canteen coupons with which they could purchase goods at the camp canteen. They were also able to place part of their earnings into a savings account. Upon repatriation, POWs received in their national currency the amount they had saved during imprisonment.

Walter recounts an act of sabotage his group carried out one day when asked to plant onion seedlings. Instead of planting the roots into the soil, Walter's POW unit stuck the green end into the ground, which enraged the farmer who threatened to have them thrown into prison. Quite often, instead of a harmless prank, the American captors viewed such behavior as an act of defiance, which it frequently was.

Walter refers to pro-Nazi POWs in the camp who made sure that "no one doubted Hitler and the eventual German victory." He relates one incident when a top Nazi POW told them to stop picking beans, arguing that they "were soldiers not bean pickers." Walter and his comrades followed the Nazis' request, as they were afraid to be put on some blacklist. The POWs' refusal to continue working almost erupted into a serious confrontation between the POWs and their captors. Only the threat of force by an American officer induced them to give in. Consequently, the unit of forty defiant POWs was transferred to Camp McAlester, Oklahoma.

The author also relates one gruesome event that made national headlines. According to his account, based on hearsay, a group of top Nazis beat to death a POW in broad daylight because they suspected this man of being a communist. Walter then claims that the Americans took the first six POWs, guilty or not, locked them up, convicted them, sentenced them to death, and hanged them outside of the camp.

What really happened, however, was that at Camp Tonkawa, Oklahoma, ideologically hardened German POWs murdered a certain Corporal Johann

Kunze after having accused him of disclosing information about German factories and military positions. American military authorities subsequently apprehended five German POWs—all veterans of the Afrika Korps—*whom they found guilty after thorough investigations and sentenced them to death. The five (not six) men were hanged at Fort Leavenworth, Kansas, in July 1945—one year after Walter had left Camp Gruber.*

Control of pro-Nazi prisoners over a large segment of the German POW population proved to be a major problem for the American authorities. Adherents to Nazi ideology frequently threatened, sometimes beat, or even killed fellow prisoners who defied them and openly demonstrated their anti-Nazi sentiment. The U.S. military attempted to solve this dilemma by separating the Nazis from the anti-Nazis. Thus, they transferred hardened Nazis to Camp Alva in Oklahoma and so-called anti-Nazis to Camps Devens (Massachusetts), Ruston (Louisiana), and McCain (Michigan), among other camps.

Camp Gruber was known as a "model camp" where many POWs, mostly from the Afrika Korps, *maintained the "German spirit," i.e., the belief in the Führer and in the superiority of the German race and* Wehrmacht *as late as the spring of 1945, when the collapse of the Nazi regime was imminent. Walter recalls a unique event, when his unit of a thousand POWs staged a "propaganda parade" in Haskell, Oklahoma, dressed in their* Afrika Korps *uniforms, marching in step, and accompanied by a regimental band that "played crisp German marches." Apparently, the townspeople lined the streets, applauding as the Germans were marching through the town. And Walter remembers that this experience "couldn't have been any better in Berlin itself." Clearly, if not the "German spirit," the POWs from the* Afrika Korps *demonstrated their elitist esprit de corps, which they had retained in captivity.*

Besides Camp Gruber, Walter stayed briefly in Camp Bixby, a branch camp near Tulsa, Oklahoma. Finally, the Army transferred Walter along with those forty obstinate POWs who had resisted military authorities in Camp Gruber to Camp McAlester, Oklahoma. There, Walter and his comrades were treated well. Their German-speaking camp commander provided them with a comfortable camp atmosphere, and they were able to establish a casual relationship with their guards despite the anti-fraternization policy imposed by the War Department. Walter recalls that for the first time "we truly realized that we were all equally human beings."

With the exception of the mentioned confrontation with the camp author-
ities in Camp Gruber, Walter has mostly good memories of his stay in
Oklahoma camps. He and his fellow POWs realized that "we considered
ourselves fortunate" while their comrades were still fighting at the front.
Certainly, German POWs in the United States lived a relatively comfort-
able life in contrast to those German soldiers who were fighting at the east-
ern front, or who starved and perished in Soviet POW camps.

— WOLFGANG T. SCHLAUCH

I wrote this report in 1996 based on my diaries and from memory. Camp
Gruber was attached to the huge American army camp of the same name,
far away from any city. Our camp was in the hollow of a gentle slope. Bare
landscape without tree or bush, nothing but sandy soil, no view of the sur-
roundings. Double barbed wire surrounded the entire camp, with high watchtowers evenly spaced. Inside, the camp was divided up into three sections,
each one of them separately fenced. Each section was intended for four companies of 250 men each. Altogether there was room for 3,000 POWs housed
in wooden barracks, with five barracks for each company, the first of which
was for non-coms.

The barracks were of lightweight construction with large windows,
unglazed but screened, and with shutters. In front and back, large gas stoves.
The paths between the barracks were wooden walkways. Each company
had a kitchen, a mess hall, and a washroom with showers, twelve washbasins with mirrors. There were two rows of toilets, but without dividers.
We would have to get used to that. We later learned that this was the usual
practice on all U.S. military bases. A general could end up sitting next to
a private.

We were divided up and moved into our barracks. We were astonished
to find Army cots, each with four blankets and a soft pillow. On every bed
there were razor, soap, comb, hand towel, and two pairs of white socks, one
size fit all, and a toothbrush with toothpaste. But shelves had apparently been
forgotten; we had to put everything on the floor. First of all, we had a good
shower; there were twelve showerheads with hot and cold water.

At noon, a gong sounded for lunch. All of us were ravenous and eager
to eat. We streamed into the mess hall, ten men to a table. And what greeted
our eyes: tables piled high with delicacies. Pork chops, all kinds of eggs,

sausages, noodles, fresh salad, corn flakes, milk, coffee, cake, different kinds of bread, and so on. We could hardly take it all in visually—and we could eat as much as we wanted. It was like the Big Rock Candy Mountain. We stuffed ourselves, but there was a lot left over. Of course we wanted to take some back to the barracks, but the KPs said no. In a couple of hours we would get just as much again. We felt we'd landed in the right place.

Life settled into a routine. Reveille at six AM, seven o'clock roll call, then breakfast, just as plentiful. Butter, milk, coffee, corn flakes, peanut butter, several flavors of jam, scrambled eggs, ham, bacon, oatmeal, rolls, several kinds of bread, etc. The roll call three times a day, when we had to form up outdoors, was always something of a problem for the guards. Although we were in rows of five, the total counts were usually different, and they had to start all over again until they agreed. It was different when an American officer took the roll call; he moved at double time along the rows and always came up with the right total. But then perhaps he didn't even really count us all. We didn't need to work during those first weeks. We slept almost all day and night.

My teeth had already been loose in Tunisia; I could wiggle them with my tongue. They got solid again, and I could again bite down and chew. I did have some trouble drinking from a cup, because my hands still shook. I went to the camp doctor every other day and had the scar tissue on my wound reduced with silver nitrate; it took almost four months. And my tooth with the temporary filling from Tunisia started to hurt. There was a dentist here, too, but all he had was pliers for extractions and couldn't make fillings. Any painful tooth he simply pulled, mine too, without anesthetic.

Both the doctor and the dentist were older men who spoke perfect German. When a sick man came to the doctor and didn't know just what was wrong, the doctor would hop up onto a small stool, then hop down again, and say, "You see, young fellow, I'm an old man, and I can still do that, so surely you aren't sick, are you?" And then the sick man was released. We presumed that the doctor was a former German Jew.

Almost every morning I woke up with a rash, which I had had as a child, but not as a soldier. It always started in the morning with itching red patches on my upper body, but went away by itself in a couple of hours. It wasn't dangerous or contagious. Any time I didn't feel like working, I went to the doctor and reported sick. If I had to wait very long, I'd rub my rash so that it wouldn't go away before I'd seen the doctor. He always applied a salve and said he was familiar with this rash, for which there was a treatment in Germany, but not yet in America.

In the summer of 1943, it was very hot in Oklahoma, and especially in our treeless camp. In the barracks, it got so hot that we couldn't sleep in them at night, so we took our mattresses outside. The night wind cooled us off a bit.

After weeks of inactivity, we were assigned to work in a rock quarry, a two-mile march on foot. The quarry was on a steep slope. We had to use hammer and chisel to break out flat stones to pave the paths in the camp. But there was no specific quota. Indeed, no one seemed to care much whether we worked or not. The whole area was fenced in with barbed wire. Several portable toilets were set up. Just beyond the lower fence began a forest, which looked like old growth. One day three Creek Indians showed up with feather headdress and fringed leather clothes, just like we had seen in picture books. They sat down on a fallen log and lit their corncob pipes. They sat there almost motionless for hours and watched us. When we started our march back to the camp, they left, too. But the next day, they were back again.

In the autumn, the farmers were able to use us for the vegetable harvest. They had planted large fields of cabbage, lettuce, spinach, and radishes. They weren't allowed to pick us up themselves, however; that would have been much too dangerous. In their eyes, all Germans were Nazi war criminals, and not even children were safe from us. In trailers, with two MPs on motorcycles and a jeep full of soldiers with machine guns aimed at us, we were transported to work. On the way back to camp, this routine was repeated. At the end of the line was the truck full of guards. This is the way we were taken to the fields. If we went through a village or town, the local police were waiting for us on motorcycles. We were moved at high speed through closed, empty streets with sirens howling. We went through Muskogee, a small town near Tulsa, almost every day. At one point, there was a movie poster in front of a theater showing Hitler on his knees lurking behind a little girl. The film was called *The Hitler Gang* [1944]. Every time we drove past, just for fun we stood at attention in the truck and saluted the poster with outstretched arms, the "Hitler salute."

Once we were taken in two large trailers to pick spinach. It was already cold and foggy in the morning. Our convoy drove along a straight highway. Apparently our driver almost missed the turn-off to the field. At the last second, he made an abrupt left turn onto a little bridge. But it was far too fast, and the trailer tipped over to the right. We all flew into the ditch, which luckily had no water in it. The following trailer was just able to stop in time. The other POWs jumped from the trailer and wanted to help us. But the guards wouldn't permit it; they held us back with their guns. We had to help ourselves. Fortunately, no one was very seriously hurt, apart from a couple of broken arms and a lot of scratches. I got hit in the back by a glass coffee maker and thought it had broken, but it hadn't.

A circle of armed guards surrounded us; no one helped us. We slowly climbed out of the ditch, and everyone checked his limbs for injuries; some of us were moaning. No one knew what to do. It was obvious that we wouldn't be picking any spinach that day. We stood or squatted there, and nothing happened, although a number of us were bleeding. Suddenly we heard sirens in the distance, and a line of ambulances and police cars arrived. Now things started to happen. Doctors in white coats and medics with stretchers ran up to us and carried the injured away. Anyone with a complaint of any kind had to get into an ambulance, including me with my back pain. This whole ambulance unit raced with sirens screaming back to Camp Gruber, not the POW camp, but rather the American Army base. They diagnosed me with some bruised ribs and ordered me to stay in bed for a week. Then we were all taken back to our camp. The others had also returned by then, and they had the day off, too.

We got 80¢ per working day, plus $3.00 a month from the German government.* This was enough to buy quite a lot in the canteen. A bar of chocolate, for example, only cost 3¢, a Coke 4¢. However, it wasn't genuine money, but rather camp scrip, plastic tokens and smaller banknotes than regular ones. Life in the camp got more interesting. Theater groups were formed and some men's choirs started rehearsing, but without any sheet music. There were supposed to be English language classes, but there weren't any books. I still had Beer's English dictionary, but it was incomprehensible to me. One of the teachers learned that I had it and asked whether I would lend it, to which I agreed, as long as I could take part in the class.

The first class started. Most of the men in the class could already speak some English from school days. I didn't learn much. Then another class was

---

* Initially POWs were paid a minimum of 80¢ a day. In the spring of 1944, the U.S. government introduced an incentive pay plan, on the basis of which a POW could earn an additional 40¢, or a total of $1.20 a day.

held, and I stayed in that one, too. This went on until I was able to speak some English. Later, it helped me a lot. Most of the other POWs refused to learn English and felt that if the Americans wanted to speak to us, they should learn German.

An unhappy chapter: there were spies among the POWs in our camp. Two-hundred-percent Nazis made sure that no one doubted Hitler and the eventual German victory, even though most of us weren't very convinced of it anymore. These spies put together secret blacklists of men who would be punished after the Germans won the war. It even got to the point where one POW who was merely suspected of having been a communist was beaten to death by a group in broad daylight. They took him between the barracks and hit him with their fists until he lay there dead. A guard in a watchtower saw what was going on and gave the alarm. The guards came running into the camp. As the group saw them coming, they quickly dispersed. The Americans grabbed the first six men they could find and locked them up, guilty or not. All of them got prison sentences. After the war, the case was opened up again, and all of them were sentenced to death and hanged in a shed outside of our camp. That was the victors' justice.

Christmas 1943 arrived. Christmas Eve isn't celebrated in America; for us it was a food festival. After a banquet, each of us got a whole pie, all of them different, with a number of delicious cakes. It was impossible to eat it all, and most of it just got thrown away. Mail from home had been held back for quite a while, but now it was distributed. Those who got something were happy, but many of us got nothing. I even got a package from my parents. There was a letter as well as some gingerbread, by now so hard that it was inedible. On the one hand, I had marvelous pies and cakes, and on the other, simple but rock-hard gingerbread that my parents had saved up for. I couldn't just throw it away. The next day, I got a pot of cocoa from the kitchen and dunked the gingerbread to soften it up. I put the pot on the stove, and filled it with gingerbread to overflowing. I took the pot from the stove, and the gingerbread was soft enough now, but I was only able to eat a couple of spoonfuls. That was enough. The rest I threw in the garbage can, with great regret.

Our Führer, Adolf Hitler, sent each POW a personal greeting in the form of an artificial fir branch with a little candle. We were very happy about this. There were German cigarettes and German tobacco in large amounts. However, by now, our smokers were long since used to the better American cigarettes and tobacco, and no one wanted the German stuff. Only one older man still smoked German tobacco. Other men left cartons of cigarettes under his bed; he had enough to last him the rest of his life.

It got cold in Oklahoma. A sharp wind blew through the camp, and there was even a light snowfall, which meant no work outdoors. We were nice and warm in the barracks with two gas stoves giving off plenty of heat in each barracks. Playing cards and chess, sleeping a lot, learning English, hearing lectures—thus the cold season passed.

Early in spring 1944, work started up again. We were taken to pick radishes for a farmer. He had a giant field and sowed one section of it early in the spring each day, another the next day, and so on. After exactly four weeks, the first section was picked, then the next. All summer long, we picked one section a day and replanted it the next. We had to bunch ten to twelve radishes together. The bunches went into a large water trough in a shed and were pulled mechanically through the water. At the end, the bunches of washed radishes fell into baskets. The farm had a railway spur of its own with a large refrigerator car waiting there every day. On one side, the radishes were loaded in by hand, and from the other, Negroes threw chipped ice over them. A day's harvest just filled a single car exactly. The radishes were taken to New York.

We also wanted to do our part for the final German victory. In the camp, we drew swastikas inside V for Victory signs on little slips of paper. We rolled these up tightly and stuck them in the freshly washed radishes. Customers in New York must have been amazed.

As POWs we were specially labeled. We had "PW" (Prisoner of War) stenciled in red on the sleeves and backs of our jackets and on our trouser legs. But now the trip to the fields wasn't so dramatic. Now there were no more sirens, just armed guards. They gradually grew less afraid of us, as they realized that we were also human beings. With time, we even got to know each other.

In the camp, we were left on our own. Americans only came into the camp for the three daily roll calls and to work in the kitchen with German assistants. Every day, large amounts of groceries were delivered and had to be consumed, no matter how. Everything had to be used up. If there were any eggs left over, they were just thrown away. If there were chops or cutlets, two large ones per person, we threw one into the garbage right in the line. We also had boiled or baked corn on the cob. At first, we refused to eat what we considered pig fodder; Germans didn't eat corn on the cob. We reluctantly tried it, though, and found that it didn't taste bad at all.

A carpentry shop was set up. In our barracks, we had an old cabinet-maker from the Black Forest who made little nightstands for us in exchange for a few cigarettes. The Americans provided plenty of wood. One empty barracks was turned into a theater with bleacher seats, a stage, and even a curtain. Here we put on plays and concerts. Of course there were no women, so men had to play these roles, which was usually very amusing.

We were permitted to mail home one letter per month, strictly censored, which usually meant that almost half of it was blacked out. But the letters did get there. For Christmas 1943, we could even pay to have our pictures taken and send the photos home. Our families could finally see what had happened to us. When we thought of our comrades at the front, we considered ourselves fortunate. We were safe here, even if it was hard to tolerate being locked up all the time. How we would have liked to be able to go out in the evening, or just be alone occasionally, but there were always other people around. Learning English was particularly difficult. There was a ditch near the fence, dug as a storm drain. Those of us learning English sat there and crammed in peace and quiet, although the sun almost baked our brains.

In the spring, we also had another job to do. A group of forty men was taken to an American military cemetery. At Fort Gibson, an hour's drive away, we had to build paths through this cemetery. This is where soldiers were buried who had been killed in action, usually about two a day. The service was very solemn. Flags were raised, and those attending the funeral arrived and conversed informally in bright clothing. They all went into a small chapel. A uniformed chaplain joined them, and everyone waited for the coffin. This was carried into the chapel and covered with a flag, and a few words were spoken. We couldn't hear what was said. The coffin was carried out on a wheeled caisson and accompanied by an honor guard to the gravesite, followed by the small funeral party. The coffin was lowered into the grave by a squeaking winch. A bugler blew "Taps," then a salute was fired, and the ceremony was over. The whole thing had barely taken five minutes, and the funeral party left the cemetery talking loudly. A few minutes later, everything was again quiet.

Every time, we stood at an appropriate distance from the grave, coming to attention as the coffin was lowered, and saluting with our hands on our caps. Every time, the funeral guests looked over at us with surprise and acknowledged our gesture. The grave was filled immediately with the excavated dirt from the next one and sown with grass, with only a small metal sign to remember the deceased. We never saw any visitors to this cemetery, although it was beautifully situated, built around a hill from which you could see a long way. The rows of graves were between trees and bushes, and on the top of the hill was the chapel. When our work there was done, we were taken to a farm to plant onions.

PLANTING ONIONS

A colored man gave each of us a wooden dibble and a bunch of seedlings; the rows were already marked out. The first man started, but stuck the green end into the ground, with the white roots sticking out. We all copied him, and no one protested, even the guards. It looked rather funny with the little roots sticking up in the air; the whole field was white instead of green.

We'd already planted a substantial area when the farmer arrived. We were curious to see what would happen. When the farmer saw our work, he clapped his hands above his head and cried, "Stop, stop! Everyone come here!" We pretended to be surprised as we came back. He yelled at our interpreter that this was sabotage, and that he would see us all thrown in prison. The interpreter naively asked whether something was wrong. The farmer almost exploded in rage. He said we'd planted the onions backwards; the roots belonged in the soil. Our interpreter responded, "What? Backwards? That's the way they plant onions in Germany. If you do it differently, I beg your pardon. Of course they'll be glad to put the roots in the ground." We could hardly contain the urge to laugh out loud, but we had to keep a straight face. From then on, we set the plants correctly.

In camp, we used some of our leisure time for crafts. Those with some talent made some lovely things. One sculptor carved a sitting lion from a large stone. The American camp commandant happened to see it and wanted it, but the sculptor wouldn't give it up. The commandant wanted to force him, but the sculptor took his hammer and smashed it. It was his lion, and no one else was going to get it. But he did offer to make the commandant a larger one. So he was allowed to go out to the quarry and find a suitable stone, which was then brought back to the camp. The sculptor made a marvelous three-foot-high sitting lion. It was his masterpiece. The commandant was very happy with it and put it in his yard.

Other men made coats-of-arms of the German administrative districts. Some of the older North Germans made canvas traveling bags out of stolen shelter halves, which they exchanged for cigarettes. From white bed sheets, they made "Africa caps" or sun hats. From one of the warehouses, I stole a shelter half, wrapping it around my body to get it out. Another POW made a big, sturdy traveling bag out of it.

Our *Afrika Korps* uniforms we kept in good condition, wearing them only on Sundays and special occasions. In the next barracks were some members of the elite Hermann Goering Division, which had relieved us in Tunisia. They hadn't been able to save the day in Africa either, despite their big mouths. One of them was Franz Ertl from the Sudetenland, near Czechoslovakia. He was a year younger than I was, with curly, light-blonde hair, and always in good spirits. We happened to end up in the same labor unit. We became friends and stayed together through almost our entire time as POWs, until we separated upon our return to Germany.

One branch camp was to be built in Bixby, Oklahoma, near Tulsa, on the Arkansas River, fifty miles away. Eighty men were transferred there, and I, too, was taken there with sixty more men on 27 March 1944. A tent camp had been set up on a farm, also surrounded with barbed wire, with German kitchen personnel. There were twelve men to a tent. The first eighty had wooden floors, but we, in the next group, didn't; our cots were on the bare ground.

It was a vegetable farm, with the farmer living on the highest point of the region in a magnificent house with a porch all the way around the house, and columns at the front entrance, from which he had a marvelous view of the farm and the area around it. Our tent camp was two hundred yards away on a smaller hill. It wasn't as comfortable as we had grown used to being, with only cold showers and less freedom of movement. The little town of Bixby was just visible in the distance. Nearby was the Arkansas River. Here we had to do the usual spring farm labor, setting onions and planting cabbage, lettuce, celery, etc. We were reasonably free, with only a single guard, and he dozed most of the time. At the end of the workday, we had to wake him up. There was also a big pond on the farm. American farm workers threw hand grenades into the pond, which brought up a lot of dead fish. These were fished out and shared with us.

A VISIT TO CAMP HASKELL

In Haskell, Oklahoma, some twenty-five miles away, there was another large POW camp we were permitted to visit one Sunday. With farm trucks, we were taken over there, accompanied by a few guards. That morning, there was a soccer match between the two camps. Then we shared a lunch with their best food. In this camp, there was even a complete German regimental band with all of its instruments. They gave a big concert in our honor.

A Protestant minister held an impressive service. We remembered our dead, prayed the war would end soon, and hoped to return home before long. Then there was a unique event. All of us together put on a propaganda parade in our full *Afrika Korps* uniforms through downtown Haskell, accompanied by the regimental band, with crisp German marches and all of us, almost one thousand men, marching in step (to the extent that our rubber soles permitted). It was very impressive, and the local population lined the streets, waved, and clapped as we passed. It couldn't have been any better in Berlin itself. Most of the people surely didn't even know who we were. But we felt like real soldiers again. That evening we returned to Bixby feeling good about ourselves.

After several days of rain, the Arkansas River overflowed its banks. The water climbed higher and higher, and soon the whole region was flooded. The quiet Arkansas became a raging torrent that pulled everything along with it. Whole Negro cabins floated by lying tilted in the water, with lots of trees and everything imaginable. The water approached our camp, too. The situation was growing critical. A tomato field we'd just planted the day before was threatened by flooding. In the pouring rain, we volunteered to go out with shovels and build a dike. As night fell, the farmers brought cars and tractors and shone their headlights on our work. We slaved away as if we were the owners, building the dike so high that no water could breach it. In the meantime, the water had reached our tents. We were on a little island and didn't know what we'd do if the water rose any higher. We couldn't reach the higher farmhouse anymore, either. It grew really eerie in the dark of night with the dirty water gurgling between the tents, and no one was able to sleep.

In the morning, the rain stopped, and the water rose no further. We breathed a sigh of relief when it grew light. The whole area was covered with water, with only the treetops showing. No one could reach us, including mail and supplies. Thank God we had enough provisions. Only two days later did the water slowly subside, leaving a layer of mud everywhere. We now wanted wooden floors for our tents, too, so we went on strike and refused to work. But that didn't work. We were taken back to the base camp and transported to various farms in the area, but we weren't punished.

We also had three Arabs from Tunisia in our camp company, who had been assigned as general assistants to some unit in Tunisia. Since they were wearing German uniforms, they ended up as POWs with us. They had a lot of difficulty making themselves understood. They could speak little German, mostly vulgar words. No one here spoke Arabic, but they could also speak some French. A German POW who spoke French tried to teach them German and English. On pieces of cardboard they hung around their necks, he wrote German and English words, which they learned as they walked around the camp. When they couldn't figure it out, they asked the first POW they saw. While showering, we learned they were circumcised, which interested us; we wanted to know how that was done. Through an interpreter, they described the process: each little boy was taken by his parents to the mosque, dressed in a kind of long, loose shirt, as is the custom there. He had to step before the imam, who stood there with a black cushion in his arms. On this cushion were pieces of gold and silver and sparkling diamonds. He stared fixedly at this splendor while his shirt was lifted and another imam quickly snipped off his foreskin with scissors. By the time he noticed what was going on, it was over, salve was applied, and a bandage. Then there was a big family party at home, but he had to stay in bed and receive his presents there.

On 4 July 1944 we again went to pick beans. The beanpoles were hanging heavy. Our quota was six bushels each, which one could easily pick in two hours. Some top Nazi in our group kept insisting we were soldiers, not bean pickers, and if they wanted beans, they should pick them themselves. Most of us didn't feel this way, though, because we also got some of the beans to eat. However, because we were afraid of getting on some blacklist, everyone went along with him. We picked one bushel and threw it onto the truck. The farmer and the guards demanded that we continue picking, but in vain. So we were taken back to camp and locked in.

Within the camp there was a stockade or guardhouse, also surrounded by its own fence. It would be crowded in there with forty men, since the six men from the murder were still in there. So we refused, on the advice of the top Nazi, to move into that barracks, since according to the Geneva Convention, there was not enough room for us all. We simply took our cots outdoors, since it was warm enough, even at night. There was only bread and water, but other POWs threw us things to eat over the fence.

POW in Oklahoma, July 1943–July 1944

The next morning, three American officers came to us and demanded that we move inside the stockade. But at the insistence of the top Nazi, we stood our ground. Our comrades on the other side of the fence encouraged us not to give in. The officers went away, so we felt we'd won. Things calmed down again. But soon we sensed tension among the Americans. We heard whistles and orders being barked. Every surrounding watchtower was outfitted with a second machine gun. Soldiers lined up all around the camp, and everyone was anxious to see what would happen next. Beyond the fence, several ambulances drove up. The main entrance was opened and a company of heavily armed troops came in wearing gas masks. Six men dressed in white set up gas canisters, and a group of medics stood by. Now things were getting serious.

The POWs near the fence picked up rocks. An officer came to us with an interpreter and demanded that we go inside the barracks within five minutes, or force would be used. Soldiers with nightsticks mingled with us. Now the risk had grown too great; we didn't want a bloodbath. As irritatingly slowly as we could move, we picked up our mattresses and entered the barracks, where there was enough room after all.

After a week, during which things weren't all that bad, thanks to the help of comrades outside who kept throwing food over the fence, we were released. But we had to pack up our belongings and were then loaded onto trucks. After a three-hour trip through endless grain and vegetable fields, we arrived in McAlester, Oklahoma, at a large but empty POW camp. A German-speaking American captain who had studied in Heidelberg was the commandant, with eight guards for the forty of us. Each of us could have had his own barracks, but we spread out in two of them. Franz Ertl and I stayed together.

The captain, who liked talking with us, promised that if we would make no trouble for him, we'd have a pretty good life here. We ate in the mess hall together with him and the eight guards. A fairly casual relationship developed between the guards and us. Here, too, we had to work in the vegetable fields, mainly picking onions. We had more than enough to eat. After work, anyone who wanted to could go into the kitchen and make himself something to eat. We had some real food orgies in that kitchen; our only condition was to leave the place clean.

A few hundred yards from the camp entrance was a public outdoor swimming pool. During the day, it was full, but at night, it was empty. We asked the camp commandant if we could use the pool when no one else was there. After some hesitation, he gave his permission, but only if we would promise to be quiet and not attempt to escape in the dark. We agreed.

Now we had to wait until the last swimmers were out of the pool, which often took quite a while. Young couples used the darkness for their own purposes. Finally it was time. All forty of us, accompanied by a couple of sentries, marched silently to the pool. It wasn't an excavated pool, but a wall built above ground and banked with dirt. Stone stairs led up to the top of the wall. The pool was in the middle of nowhere, easily accessible, with the nearest houses quite far away.

From the camp spotlights came some illumination, but it was dark otherwise. Of course we had no bathing trunks, but that was no problem. We climbed the steps naked and dived into the pool. The guards had to look after our clothes. But they couldn't take it for long. Suddenly, they got undressed and jumped into the pool with us. The water was just deep enough for us to stand up in. There were lots of water fights and no differences between our guards and us now. For the first time, we truly realized that we were all equally human beings. After an hour of fooling around, we'd had enough. All of us got out of the pool and put on only our underpants and carried our clothes back, while the guards had to tug their uniforms back on without drying off first. During all of this, the commandant had watched from a distance and seemed quite satisfied with us; from then on, he allowed us to use the pool every evening.

Sadly, this pleasant time was soon over. By now, we had become like a big family. The guards weren't afraid of us, nor we of them. Since my English was now adequate, I often talked with them. We didn't like having to leave this camp, but on 25 July 1944 we were taken back to Camp Gruber. The very next day came the order to get ready for another transport by rail, not just us; this time it was four hundred men.

———

The Land of Enchantment — POW in Las Cruces, New Mexico, July 1944–March 1946

INTRODUCTION

*W*alter Schmid vividly describes his train ride from Oklahoma through Texas, Santa Fe, and then along the Rio Grande to Las Cruces, located in southern New Mexico. Along with about 340 fellow POWs, Walter was transferred to the downtown camp, one of the two camps in the city. Since the fall of 1943, these two camps had housed hundreds of Italian POWs, who had been transferred a few weeks before the arrival of Walter's group.

Walter mentions his experience as a field-worker: chopping and picking cotton; harvesting cantaloupes, onions, and vegetables; and cleaning irrigation ditches. Based on his diary, Walter started out picking only sixty pounds of cotton on his first day, increased his output to 101 pounds on the second

41

day, and to 151 pounds two weeks later. He exceeded the required quota of 210 pounds, imposed by the camp commander, on forty-two days between October and December 1945. All together, he harvested more than 36,000 pounds of cotton during two seasons in 1944–1945 and 1945–1946. Walter's high productivity defies frequent complaints by farmers and military officials who rightly claimed that the performance of POWs in comparison to "free labor" was considerably lower. Walter seems to have been an exception as he even outproduced many of his own comrades.

The author highlights the development of a friendship between himself and several Mexican-American teenage boys who worked with the German POWs in the fields. He recalls the kindness of a Japanese-American farmer and his family, for whom he and his fellow POWs worked. And he mentions a small farmer and his wife, who, initially quite reserved, became increasingly friendly toward the prisoners. These and other positive experiences with the civilian population were in contrast to the U.S. government–imposed anti-fraternization rule, which, however, was frequently ignored by civilians as well as by military personnel.

Walter's comment that "Mexicans and blacks in N.M. were second class citizens, regarded [by Americans] merely as cheap labor" was an observation shared by many POWs. In particular those working in the South observed racial discrimination toward blacks. Quite frequently, they applied this criticism to counter Allied condemnation of Nazi racist ideology. Many of the POWs, however, especially those who were captured during the latter part of the war, could not have been oblivious of the fact that the Nazi regime exploited millions of Eastern Europeans and Jews as slave laborers in war industries and agriculture throughout Germany and German-occupied Europe, millions of whom died of exhaustion and starvation.

The author is critical of his camp commander, Captain Clark D. Williams. He describes him as a violent man who humiliated the POWs and imposed heavy penalties on those who did not fulfill their quota. He relates that in addition to an empty barracks that was converted into a stockade, Captain Williams had a small cage constructed where he could lock up one prisoner at a time. The individual would then be exposed to the sun, was given little food to eat, and had to sleep on the ground.

Can these and additional severe allegations against Captain Williams be corroborated? A number of surviving POWs who were interviewed generally confirm accusations made by Schmid. Significantly, an International

Red Cross inspection team came to a similar conclusion. In their report of their April 1945 visit, they were critical of the excessively harsh penalties levied by Captain Williams, which, as they emphasized, did not conform to the Geneva Convention. They also mentioned the barbed-wire cage where a POW, depending on the gravity of his offense, could be placed for one to two weeks, getting food only every three days, and receiving no blankets, which forced him to sleep on the bare ground. They concluded that the camp commandant had little sensitivity toward the POWs. As Captain Williams "categorically refused to modify his viewpoint," the delegation submitted its report to the commanding officer of the base camp in Fort Bliss, Texas. After their next visit, at the beginning of 1946, a few weeks before the POWs were returned to Europe, the same delegation reported that the conditions had improved, the number of penalties was greatly reduced, and the cage had been removed.

Some of these statements made by Walter Schmid against the camp commandant, such as Captain Williams "pocketing money" that the POWs were supposed to have received, or his claim that the U.S. Army court-martialed Captain Williams after the war, cannot be confirmed. Moreover, in defense of Captain Williams, statements by both POWs and the International Red Cross indicate that concerning discipline, he was as strict with American personnel as with POWs.

Walter's observation that the guard units were "not made up of the best soldiers," but of men who "hadn't amounted to much in the Army," requires clarification. The army initially used some guard personnel who lacked the necessary experience and training in dealing with POWs. Later, men who were wounded in action or had been in German POW camps, some of whom resented the German POWs, did guard duty. Finally, few guards were able to speak German, which impeded their communication with the POWs. Eventually, proper training of personnel improved the quality of the guard units.

Walter mentions that after the end of the war in Europe, food rations for the POWs were drastically reduced. He and his comrades were not alone in experiencing shortages of food. Due to protests by American civilians who felt that the POWs were "coddled" and fed too well, the War Department had ordered the cutting back of rations in the POW camps in September 1944. Additional reductions took place in February 1945, due to the decline of food supplies and an increase in their demand for the U.S.

Army. After V-E Day, with further reduction of POW menus, the POWs believed that these measures were based on the revelations of the mistreatment of American POWs in Germany as well as the liberation of Nazi concentration camps, which revealed the horrific crimes carried out by the Nazis. In most POW camps, however, the food supply returned to normal after a few weeks. Walter surmises correctly that since the farmers expected greater productivity for their money, their camp commander started to feed the POWs better.

Like most POWs, Walter and his fellow POWs had to watch documentary films about the liberated concentration camps, events that were incomprehensible to him. He states that they had known nothing about these camps, but agrees that they as Germans should be ashamed of those deeds. Though members of the Afrika Korps *might not have known details about these camps, they had seen numerous acts of persecution of Jews by the Nazis, such as the* Kristallnacht *of November 1938.*

In March 1946, Walter and his fellow POWs packed up to leave the Las Cruces Camp. Their train ride to New York and their voyage across the Atlantic to Europe were a joyous affair. They expected to be soon repatriated and looked forward to returning to their homes after almost three years of captivity. — WOLFGANG T. SCHLAUCH

It was a two-day trip by train across Oklahoma, Texas, and New Mexico, along the Rio Grande, finally arriving in Las Cruces, forty-five miles north of El Paso. We saw a lot of varied scenery while traveling through the grain belt of mid-America, right during harvest time. Here we saw for the first time giant combines working in gangs of up to ten. They worked all through the night, with lights everywhere in the darkness. They did not mow the grain even with the ground, but at the height of the ears.

Fertile plains alternated with stony desert, with little towns between them, with their brightly painted wooden houses. Between the houses and the streets, no fences or walls or vegetable gardens, just green lawns. But then the landscape changed as we got to the Rio Grande. The soil, the fields, even the houses, everything was reddish-brown. In Santa Fe, the train stopped to take on water, since the steam-driven locomotive used a lot of water. The roof tanks on the cars were also refilled. The city of Santa Fe didn't look like other American towns. Its magnificent houses were made of red-brown adobe clay, although we could only tell that by looking closely. From there, we traveled along the Rio Grande through a fertile valley in which mainly cotton was planted. Sometimes the valley was narrow, sometimes miles wide. The single-spur train track went right through the fields without any real embankment. The tracks were simply laid on ties in the sand, and so the cars wobbled back and forth.

All four hundred men got out in Las Cruces, a small town in New Mexico. After a short march, we entered a camp between what is today Melendres Street and the train tracks, about half a mile south of the train station. But this camp was much different than all the others. There was no fence; everything was open, and right on the edge of town! There were five big, long barracks in the middle of a green lawn, with silvery poplars all over the area—it was a real idyll, and this was where we were going to live. We were greeted by Captain Williams, our new camp commandant, but his first order was to prohibit us from leaving the camp and going into town. Some of us didn't follow that order, so a nine-foot barbed-wire fence was erected around the whole camp with a high wooden watchtower at each corner; now it was a regular POW camp.

Today's Melendres Street, on which our camp stood, was just a dusty gravel road then, without any houses between Main Street and our camp, just cotton fields. We moved into the barracks, with a broad aisle down the middle and wooden beds on each side, without mattresses, but with five olive-drab quilts and one pillow each. Outside of the barracks were washrooms and showers, and upstairs the usual toilets, not quite as comfortable as Camp Gruber.

We found out that this camp had been built for migrant Mexican farm workers who came over for the cotton harvest every year. We were apparently going to take their place. Here in the broad Rio Grande Valley, cotton seemed to be the principal crop, along with melons and, mainly on the Stahmann Farms, pecans; a gigantic area was planted with nothing but these nut trees.

Captain Williams, our camp commander, had been born in France and was a short, stocky man with a thin mustache.★ He chewed tobacco and spit it in thin streams on the ground. His short black stubble and his cold,

---

★ Captain Williams was born in New Castle, Indiana, in 1911, not in France.

piercing eyes made him unpleasant to look at. He had been assigned the post of POW camp commandant by the Army. We got to know him as a violent man who was only interested in us as labor, from which he apparently earned some money. In the camp itself, he more or less left us in peace, but everyone was afraid of him, even his own soldiers.

Fritz Kehrer from Neckarweihingen was chosen as the German camp leader. He was twenty-two years old. Although he had graduated from high school, he hadn't become an officer. His father had been murdered in a concentration camp. He was a quiet man and always did his best for us, and of course, he spoke English fluently.

The cotton picking hadn't begun yet, so the farmers came and picked us up to help with plowing and other jobs. The cotton is sown anew every year in rows, which are then piled up, and the field has to be watered every five to six days. For the purposes of irrigation, the Rio Grande is dammed north of Las Cruces at the Elephant Butte Lake, making the river here about as broad as the Neckar River in Germany. The water is then conducted across country in big canals, which branch off into ever smaller ones until they come to the heads of the fields. The fields are all leveled, so that opening the sluice gates makes the water flow into the plowed rows until they're full.

Every morning, the farmers arrived at seven o'clock in all kinds of vehicles. We had already been divided up into groups, according to how many each farmer had requested, and were waiting at the gate. Upon leaving the camp, each POW was frisked by a guard to keep him from smuggling anything out, and this procedure was repeated when we returned. But with time, we figured out ways to smuggle things.

One farmer wanted us to weed the rows between the knee-high cotton plants. A worker took us to the field and distributed hoes. We started to chop up the soil thoroughly, carefully working around each cotton plant, just as they do in Germany. The field was more than a mile long; we couldn't see the other end. The sun shone mercilessly, and we didn't dare take off our shirts. We hadn't gotten very far when the farmer showed up around noon. He yelled at us to stop and to come back. This was sabotage, he said, and it would cost him too much. Quit work, he said, and get into the truck. We looked at each other uncomprehendingly; none of us knew what was going on or what he meant. We were taken back to camp, Captain Williams listened to the farmer's complaints, and we were immediately locked up. One of the empty barracks was used as a stockade. We still had no idea why, because we hadn't been doing a bad job.

We couldn't just swallow this punishment, so we had our German camp leader Fritz Kehrer tell the captain we weren't aware of having done anything wrong, and we wanted to know why we had been locked up. The answer was, we hadn't accomplished enough, but we argued against that and said they should show us how to do it better. The next day, the farmer himself picked us up. When we got to the field, he took a hoe under his arm and marched ahead. When he saw a weed while he was walking, he chopped it off; there was almost no weed left. So that's the way it's done, we learned.

HEALTH CHECK

Something unusual was introduced here, too, a health check, or at least that's what they called it. One Sunday or Monday a month, all four hundred men had to line up in spread-out rows in the roll-call square. Everyone had to take down his pants and stand there half-naked. An older, German-speaking doctor showed up, accompanied by our captain and two armed guards. The doctor was a German Jew. He bent down in front of each man; each of us had to pull back his foreskin, and the doctor squeezed the head of each penis to see if there was any dripping that might indicate a venereal disease. There never was a single case.

At first, this was an embarrassing ritual for us, since civilians could see us, what with our camp lying right on the single-spur train track to El Paso. Passenger trains still ran back then, and the passengers could also see us, but we eventually got used to this, too. One POW, however, who had arrived later, had been a medical student, and he wouldn't put up with the treatment. When the doctor wanted to check him, he slapped his fingers away. The startled doctor jumped back, and the two guards ran up and held the student's arms. Everyone was tense, and the captain stood there not knowing what to do. We were afraid something terrible would happen. Then the student started screaming that this was disgusting; any real doctor would know he should wash his hands after each contact, and the whole business was a matter for the Red Cross.

The captain just stood there, not understanding the complaint, but when an interpreter explained it to him, he stopped the examination. There were no repercussions. The examinations still continued every month, but now we only lowered our pants when the doctor approached, and we pulled back our own foreskins and squeezed our own penises. Either they had wanted to humiliate us, or both of them were homosexuals; nothing like this was done in any other camp.

If one of us got seriously ill, beyond the resources of our medics, he was taken down to El Paso to a hospital. Dental work was done there, too. The practice with American dentists at the time was simply to pull a tooth if the patient complained of pain, rather than treating it, as in Germany. But there were now also German dentists in El Paso, together with the American ones, and they treated the teeth and filled them, rather than pulling them immediately. The Americans learned something from this.

Our captain decided at one point that our hair was too long. It was only supposed to be as long as a matchstick, just as in the German army, but no one paid much attention to this any more. One evening during roll call before supper, he came into camp, walked down the rows and checked out each man's hair length. Anyone whose hair was too long had to step forward, which meant almost all of us. A rope was tied around the entire group, and we were told that no one could get out until he had short hair. Guards with guns watched us. There we stood, hungry, and had to get our hair cut. The camp barber started to give us rough haircuts, but this would have taken forever with several hundred men. I remembered my fingernail scissors and called to one of my friends who wasn't tied in the group to go get them. He threw them to me, and I started to cut the long curly hair of my friend Ertl. Then it was my turn, and afterward we both looked terrible, but we'd done what we'd been told to do, so we were free and could go to supper. I left my scissors with the others. Not until after midnight did the last men have short haircuts. In the following days, the barber gave us a somewhat more humane appearance.

The Organ Mountains, a lovely mountain range east of Las Cruces, were always in view while we worked. They were also our means of orientation. Two of the Austrian POWs in our camp were enthusiastic mountain climbers, for whom the mountains were a beckoning goal. One day, they reported to the captain and asked him for permission to do a rock climb some Sunday in the Organs. The captain looked at them incredulously. "Why in the world would you want to go up there? They're just bare rock!" They just wanted to go climbing and enjoy the view from the top, they said, and they definitely wouldn't try to escape. He said he'd make the view easier for them—he'd get them some aerial photographs. No, that wasn't what they wanted; they just wanted to do some rock climbing. He said he personally would allow it, but something like that was simply forbidden (our captain was actually fairly flexible when it didn't have to do with labor). However, if they could talk a guard into going with them, it was all right with him. But that was the end of their plan, because they couldn't find any guard who was willing to accompany them on such an unusual trip. The captain seemed not to have been concerned about them escaping, but if there had been an accident, he would have been held responsible.

An aunt of our German camp leader, Kehrer, who had married an American and lived in the U.S.A., came to visit him one day in camp. This was a big event for Kehrer and a welcome break in our routine that he was able to recall fondly for a long time.

COTTON PICKING

The cotton harvest started on 21 September 1944. The cotton plants were now as tall as we were, with the cotton bolls opened, so that the cotton burst out in five strands and hung there. A skilled twist could remove the cotton from the boll. It was then stuck into a six-foot sack tied to the picker's body and dragged along between his legs. It had to be done in a single move, without having to pull twice; otherwise, time would have been wasted, and in America, time is money.

The first day, I managed to pick sixty pounds. The cotton was weighed by the sack and paid for by the pound, so I made 32¢. But the next day, I picked 101 pounds and got credit for 61¢. I increased my yield until I got to 150 pounds in early October. But our captain still thought this wasn't enough. He demanded that we pick much more. The farmer paid any picker, whether he was black, Mexican, or one of us, $3.00 for 100 pounds. A full sack weighed about seventy-five pounds, including the cottonseed. The seeds are removed at the cotton gin and make a good oil, similar to olive oil. But we only got 60¢ for the same amount. Part of that the captain almost certainly pocketed, so he was intent on increasing our productivity.★ Crowds of Mexicans and colored men from nearby Mexico also came for the cotton harvest. They had their certain specific farms they came to every year.

★ This cannot be confirmed. In fact, the POWs' "Pay Records" seem to indicate that the POWs were fully paid, including the additional incentive pay of 40¢ per day.

With everything they owned, whole families lived in trailers or tents, right at the fields. Everyone helped with the harvest; even the smallest children got a small sack tied on. The amount they earned in about five months allowed them to live decently in Mexico for the rest of the year. They had very modest needs. They got water from the ditches, where there were also fish, frogs, chile peppers, and other wild plants.

Of course it was very hot in the cotton fields, without any breeze between the six-foot plants. We had to work along each row bent over, with the sun burning on our backs and our throats drying out. As the sack was filled, it grew harder to drag it along. A large water barrel was set up to quench our thirst; it was filled to the brim and a couple of blocks of ice floated in it, which kept the water cool until evening. However, so that not every picker had to go to the barrel, a water boy was employed to bring water in a smaller container to the workers. We just had to call out "Agua, agua!" and he would come, or maybe not. But the water wasn't drunk out of cups. You poured it from a ladle into your open mouth from above, which took a few tries to master. This was a hygienic solution, with no one's mouth touching the ladle. Most of the time, we worked together in a field with the Mexicans and blacks. At a large farm like the Stahmann Farm we had to work hardest. Between the still small pecan trees, cantaloupes had been planted, which were harvested in May and June.

A group of Mexican-Americans worked together with us. I often had conversations with them. In several English classes that had been offered at Camp Gruber, I'd learned enough English to be able to talk to children. At school, Mexican-American children have to learn English; their first language is Spanish. Older people can't speak any English, and young people speak only Spanish among themselves. One thirteen-year-old Mexican-American boy, Junior Barela, who lived with his family in the middle of Stahmann Farm, was a quiet kid. Unlike his friends, who were always in a cheerful mood, he always had a serious expression on his face and was rather shy, with dark brown eyes and long, black hair.

He liked to talk to me and was very curious and eager to learn; he always tried to work next to me in the cotton fields. Even if his people had already started work, he'd pick another row with me. When he saw me coming, he'd call out from a distance for me to join him. His parents found this amusing. If we were first, I'd do an extra row with him, too. He liked being on the dividing line between the natives and us. The other POWs turned up their noses at my spending time with people like that, but I liked the chance to use my English and improve it. And I learned a lot about how the Mexicans lived and thought. I became a real friend to this young boy. I got along well with his brother, a year older, and Philip Guzman, from Las Cruces, and Ernesto Padilla from Mesilla; they were all about fourteen. We soon got to be friends, although we only saw each other at work. This friendship was a kind of small freedom for me. To spend almost three years with the same men in a very small space can be quite frustrating.

Mexicans and blacks in New Mexico were second-class citizens, regarded merely as cheap labor. They were used to this and made the best of it. The children left school at twelve or thirteen; why stay in school if they were just going to be cheap labor for the white farmers, like their parents? For a week's work, they got $36.00 apiece, no matter how old they were. The cotton was paid by weight. They spent their wages the following week; no one had heard of saving money. We even saw elderly people who could hardly walk still working in the fields. I asked why and was told they needed the money to subsist, since there were no pensions or old-age insurance in America.

When I asked Junior once whether he'd saved anything up, he looked at me quizzically. Why, he wondered? There's more money every week. They didn't need much to live on, and with the whole family working, as was usually the case, they could easily have saved some money. They didn't spend much on clothing, just trousers and shirts, which they wore almost until they fell off. Most of the time they went barefoot and only wore old sandals for special kinds of work.

They lived in one-story flat-roofed homes made of dried clay mixed with straw, painted white. These houses were cool inside when it was hot and pleasantly warm in wintertime. Most houses only had a single room where everything took place. The children heard whatever was going on between the parents. Most cooking was done outdoors.

One morning, Willie Barela, Junior's older brother, showed up for work looking very dejected, and I asked him what the matter was. He told me he'd lost his wallet with his whole week's wages. I felt very sorry for him. But then he came back that afternoon grinning from ear to ear—he'd found it. Where? I asked him. In bed, he said; it must have slipped out of his trousers pocket. I wanted to know if he took off his trousers in bed. He looked at me with an odd expression; why take off your trousers when you're just going to have to put them back on in the morning?

Junior was very curious and wanted to know all about me, such as where I was from and why I was here. He'd heard about a war somewhere or other. But "Germany" was meaningless to him. Nor could he understand why we would go to war if we had everything we needed. He couldn't figure out why they had to go to war just like white people, even though they were second-class citizens. Young white men liked young Mexican girls as girl-friends, but they would never marry them. However, if the Mexicans approached a white girl, their lives were in danger. If they went into a tavern where there were whites, they got kicked right out. All these injustices, which his friends didn't even notice any more, he just couldn't understand.

I asked him what he did with his money every week. He said he went to the movies, bought liquor and cigarettes, and paid for girls. When he needed new clothes (the old ones were rarely washed, much less mended), he'd go to a store, buy a shirt or trousers, change into them in the dressing room, and just leave his old clothes there. A shirt or pair of trousers cost two dollars each. Every farmer and white man wore the same thing; even the army had the same clothes.

During the tedious work in the cotton fields, the Mexicans liked to sing. Melancholy songs alternated with fast, rhythmic tunes. There were some gifted musicians among the singers, especially the tenors, each one better than the one before him. We all liked to listen to them.

From time to time, we could tell the Mexicans were growing restless in the fields. They'd untie their cotton sacks and disappear. Far away from us, they'd then form a circle. In the six-foot-high cotton, all we could see was the tops of their heads. Soon thereafter we'd hear rhythmic clapping and cries of encouragement. But when we tried to come closer to see what was going on, the otherwise friendly Mexicans and our guards would chase us away relentlessly. Then after half an hour, they'd come back and start work again without a word.

I asked my young friend what that was all about. He said, "I can't tell you. It's a strict secret." "You can tell me; I won't tell anyone else." "Young couples make love, and everyone urges them on." I stared at him incredulously. "It's completely natural, and it's a lot of fun," he said. "How about you?" I asked, "Do you do that, too?" "I'd like to," he answered, "but I don't have a girlfriend—still, I can learn a lot by watching."

One overcast day when the sun wasn't shining, we saw that all the Mexicans were depressed. They weren't singing, and they seemed reluctant to work. I asked Junior what was wrong; had someone died? "No, but look—the sun isn't shining, and we can't live without the sun." Even though they complained about the heat of the day, they didn't want to be without sunshine.

One time we took our noon break near a canal that had been dammed up. It was a perfect place for a swim. The Mexicans had gone home for lunch, and we were alone except for the guard, and no one was worried about him. All forty of us decided to take a dip. Naturally, we didn't have swim trunks with us, so in we went naked, and did it feel marvelous! All of a sudden, we saw a bunch of apples floating toward us. They could only have been meant for us, and we caught all of them, one apiece. We looked for the generous donor, but could only see something white in the bushes. We climbed out of the water to see what it was. There stood two young ladies waving at us. We, in all our naked glory, waved back gratefully.

On 29 October 1944, all of us were ordered to donate blood. A row of high tables was set up, on which we placed our right arms. American medics took the blood, usually until they saw that the donor was about to keel over, which some of us actually did. Allegedly, it was needed for our own German wounded.

Another day we were out picking cotton when we heard a loud droning that grew steadily more deafening, as a B-17 Flying Fortress bomber came flying low right toward us. We froze in panic as it flew right over our heads, and a sack of money fell at our feet. Was it for us? Then we saw the farmer come running across the field to grab the moneybag.

On 3 December 1944 there was a thorough physical exam, and not just penises this time. We were divided up into groups, and I was in Group A. What purpose the exam had, we were never told.

ONE GUARD

We got along pretty well with the guards as a rule. As time passed, we got to know each other. Usually, only one of them accompanied us to work, and he didn't pay much attention to us—with the exception of one particular guard. He was an Indian, although he wore an American uniform; one could see his Indian facial features. He always behaved like God Almighty, but he was really just a bit mentally retarded. Every group crossed itself when he stood guard in the field. If anyone even threw eggshells or orange peels on the ground during lunch break, as we usually did, he would insist on us picking them all up and depositing them somewhere else. We couldn't go off to relieve ourselves, as we ordinarily did, but had to report to him first. He would then go along, whether it was for defecating or urinating, and stand with his rifle leveled at the man, until we were done.

Naturally, we riled him whenever we could. For example, if we would all report to relieve ourselves at the same time, he would go crazy. He could only deal with one of us at a time. We threatened to tell the captain, because we often didn't manage to go to the bathroom in time and had to urinate in our pants.

We soon learned that the guard units were usually not made up of the best soldiers, but rather men who hadn't amounted to much in the army. For guard duty in a POW camp, they were good enough. The guards were just as afraid of the captain as we were. He was very strict with them, too, which usually got taken out on us.

Another time we were lucky with our Indian. It was a very hot day, and everyone was looking for a shady spot for our noon break. The guard took off his shirt, lay down, and quickly nodded off with his rifle lying next to him. In the distance, we saw a jeep stirring up a dust cloud; that could only be the captain, and here was our guard, fast asleep. We were tempted to leave him be and see what would happen. It was our noon break, so there was nothing he could do to us, but the guard would surely be in serious trouble. But then one of us felt sorry for him and said we had to wake him up. The jeep was getting closer and closer. We woke him, and he jumped up and grabbed his rifle, but he didn't have his shirt on. He was so muddled that he couldn't figure out what to do next. We pulled him behind the cotton wagon, took his rifle strap off his shoulder, put on his shirt, fastened his belt buckle, and put on his helmet. All of us helped, and he just stood there and let us dress him. At the very moment the captain arrived, we were finished and were able to push him forward. He could report that everything was fine. The captain didn't notice a single thing and drove away. The guard never thanked us, but from then on, he was a changed man with us. The other groups just couldn't figure out what had happened.

RANCHER MANDEL

A rancher named Mandel used us for a week. It was a half-hour drive toward El Paso on the west side. It wasn't for cotton picking this time; we were brought in to clean up his neglected ranch. Around his house was a sizeable cattle ranch; he didn't even know for sure how many head of cattle he had. A couple of bulls provided for plenty of calves. The ranch extended down to the Rio Grande, where the cattle would drink.

Occasionally, he'd sell a truckful of cattle. Some of them died and were just left lying where they fell. Bleached ribs were all over the place. There were a few cows in the stall for daily milking. There was an apparatus to combat the swarms of flies; an electrically charged screen attracted them, and when they touched it, they were zapped with a tiny blue flame. A little cloud of smoke rose, which in turn drew more bugs.

Mandel's ancestors had come from Germany, but he didn't speak German anymore. His wife was a schoolteacher in El Paso; they had no children, but lived alone on this big ranch.

The fences needed repairing, the farm implements had to be maintained and spruced up, the house needed painting, and so on. These were jobs for our skilled craftsmen; here they could show what they could do. A lot of materials were needed, so Mandel just sent one of us in his car to the next town to pick things up. One young POW truck driver could already speak good English; he picked up what was needed and put it on the rancher's bill.

We were all really excited about this project. The rancher left everything to us while he stood around happily and watched. Every evening, he would proudly show his wife what we had accomplished. After a week, the place looked like new. At first, Mandel had been quite reserved, but as he got to know us, he grew steadily friendlier. For our lunch break, he'd bring us a can of fresh milk.

OUR MUSICAL BAND

The year 1944 drew to a close, and the news from Germany kept getting worse. German cities were being bombed without interruption, and many of them lay in smoking ruins. Most POWs weren't getting mail any more. The promised "wonder weapon" was now regarded skeptically even by the big Nazis in the camp; they grew quieter and quieter. No trace of blacklists now. Christmas was celebrated quietly, but the desire for a camp band was growing. Our camp leader Kehrer sent around a request for anyone who could play an instrument, and I signed up to play the trumpet.

One guard who had played as a musician for MGM in Hollywood was able to obtain some used instruments inexpensively. They were paid for from the canteen's surplus earnings, which raised our prices a bit. We got two trumpets, a piano, a big drum set, two saxophones, several violins and guitars, and an accordion as a start. The guard was even able to get us sheet music for the latest American tunes from Hollywood through his MGM connections. But he could only get us the piano score, so we had to write out our own parts and transpose them where necessary. We practiced conscientiously in our free time and were soon able to give our first concert.

We also had music for a lot of old German songs. We ended every outdoor concert with either "The Stars of Home" [Heimat deine Sterne] or "At the End of Another Lovely Day" [Wieder geht ein schöner Tag zu Ende]. There were usually a lot of moist eyes, especially when the trumpets played a solo. My fellow trumpeter from Pforzheim was a splendid musician. He played first trumpet, and I played second. Our camp leader Fritz Kehrer was a fine sax player.

At one sunset concert, everything started out fine. But after the sun went down, the strings got more and more out of tune. Retuning didn't improve matters. One after another had to give up and quit. The piano also sounded terrible. Only the trumpets had no problems. What was going on? we wondered. We finally figured it out. As soon as the sun had set, it cooled off enough for the strings to lose their tuning. From then on, we only played when it was still light.

Surprisingly, the captain gave us a completely free hand with our concerts. He came to almost every concert we gave outdoors, and the guards never missed one. The captain must have been somewhat proud to have a band like this in his camp, at least as long as our work output was high.

We musicians regularly gathered around the PA system microphone before lights out and played some evening serenades. Here was the program of our concert for Sunday, 8 April 1945. We started with the usual fanfare, then

1. "Swing the Swing"
2. "Sweet Dreams, Sweetheart"
3. "Aloha Oe"
4. "Waiting"
5. "My Sweetheart Must Be a Sailor" [Mein Schatz muss ein Matrose sein]
6. "Candy"

7. "Looking Out the Window" [Fenstergucker]
8. "Czardas" [Hungarian dance]
9. "Quicksilver Polka"

INTERMISSION

10. "Barcelona"
11. "Magic in the Moonlight"
12. "My Heart Belongs to You"
    [Dein ist mein ganzes Herz]
13. "Poinciana"
14. piano solo (ten minutes of Peter [playing] Mozart)
15. "La Paloma"
16. "Besame mucho"
17. "Accordiana"
18. "Moonlight and Roses"
19. "Into Each Life Some Rain Must Fall"
20. "Santa Lucia"
21. "The Village Goes to Sleep"
    [Die kleine Stadt will schlafen gehn]
22. "The End of Another Lovely Day"
    [Und wieder geht ein schöner Tag zu Ende]

Our thanks was thunderous applause. Sadly, we were unable to take our instruments home to Germany.

In early February, the cotton-picking was finished. The unopened bolls were picked up. The dried-up plants were chopped up and plowed under as fertilizer. The soil was disked, and new cottonseed was sown.

My totals were 3,476 lbs. of cotton for October and 3,512 lbs. for November. We were glad to be able finally to do other kinds of work. The farmers and ranchers picked us up mostly to clean out and maintain the irrigation ditches.

One old bowlegged farmer took a group to his farm near Anthony, which was quite a ways away and close to the mountains. With his ancient Ford and a rickety trailer, he set out with twelve of us and built up considerable speed on the road. The worn-out trailer swayed from side to side, and we got more and more scared to death that it was going to tip over.

We yelled to him as loudly as we could to slow down, but neither he nor our guard sitting next to him heard a thing. Maybe they thought we were just yelling for joy or something. We had to do something to keep from tipping over, so one of us took the five-gallon glass coffee pot and threw it forward onto the top of the car, where it shattered into a thousand pieces. Then the driver stopped and asked, in a surprised voice, what was wrong. We explained it to him, and then he drove more slowly, quite unconcerned about the dent in the roof of his car.

At his little farm in the valley, we met his equally bowlegged wife. She greeted us with a nod, wearing a battered old cowboy hat on her sparse hair. We noticed there were many more cars and trucks standing around than two old people could possibly have used. Since one of us happened to be an auto mechanic, he asked the farmer what he did with all those vehicles. He said none of them ran anymore, but he didn't know what was wrong with them. When one of them quit running, he'd just leave it there and buy another one.

This whetted our mechanic's curiosity, and he asked if he could take a look at them. He saw immediately that only minor things were wrong with the vehicles, so he offered to fix them. The farmer seemed pleased and told him if he needed any spare parts, he could take the old Ford into town and get what he needed. Our mechanic set right to work while the farmer assigned us ditch-maintenance jobs. During the next few days, our mechanic repaired every vehicle with a minimum of parts and tools. The farmer and his wife smiled broadly and were obviously overjoyed. All of us had a good time with them.

WHO'S A NAZI?

Our Captain Williams had us line up for roll call on 22 March 1945 and gave a speech that the interpreter had to translate for us. He asked for anti-Nazis to inform him in writing. Well, the concepts "Nazi" and "anti-Nazi" didn't even exist for us. We were just German soldiers and POWs. Not one of us wrote to him, whereupon our captain declared the entire camp a Nazi camp, with all the consequences this implied. Our camp leader Kehrer now had to be personally responsible for order. This was a real burden for him, and he didn't think he'd survive it with everything that had already happened in the camp. He even gave away all his personal belongings. Then came the end of the war, which was feared by us all.

THE END OF THE WAR: 7 MAY 1945

On the morning of 7 May 1945, the entire camp was called out. We weren't sent to work. The captain again gave a speech, and the interpreter translated. We Germans had just lost the war we had started. As of now, the Geneva Convention (for the protection of POWs) no longer applied to us. (That was a violation of international law by self-righteous America.) Now we would be subject to any whim, since we were all considered Nazis. We suspected bad things, knowing this captain.

The first severe measure was the removal by truck of all supplies and groceries from kitchen and canteen. There was now no more food in the kitchen and nothing to eat. Most of us had a small supply of chocolate and candy, but these were soon gone. We couldn't work anymore; otherwise we might have been able to forage for something to eat. These were tough days for us, and our stomachs growled constantly. All we had was water and hunger.

Finally, after five days of starving, we got a thin cabbage soup. And on 15 May, we were again allowed to work, but without lunch. We were hardly able to work, we were so weak.

Again, we went to the Stahmann Farm, where my friend Junior and other friends were working. He was very happy to see me again. But then he noticed during our noon break that we didn't have anything to eat and were just sitting around. He asked me why, and I told him. He thought about this as he looked at me, then quietly went home. Soon he came back and signaled to me to meet him apart from the others. When we were by ourselves, he gave me a package wrapped in newspaper. He had brought me a burrito, a kind of thin pancake with ground beef, scrambled eggs, and spicy sauce wrapped up in it. I had to eat it in secret, and it tasted wonderful, although a bit spicy for my taste. From then on, he brought me one every day. The other POWs didn't notice a thing. He didn't stop until we were getting enough to eat once more. That kid was a real friend. Sadly, I couldn't pay him back, but I never have forgotten his help.

Gradually we started getting enough to eat again. The farmers seemed to have encouraged the captain to feed us better, because they wanted more work from us for their money. The canteen reopened, too. We wanted to be able to spend our money here. We still only had plastic tokens instead of real dollars and could only spend this money in the camp. In addition to candy, ice cream, and canned beer, there were now rings, silver jewelry, Indian-made leather goods, and underwear.

And the food got steadily better. We were allowed to plant a vegetable garden between our camp and the Las Cruces train station at Court and Melendres streets, so we now had fresh produce, too. The situation would have been tolerable if only there hadn't been such enormous pressure on us to work harder. The captain was relentless about that.

MELON HARVEST

The owner of Stahmann Farm was a very wealthy man. His farm was enormous, and he was said to own two more just like this one. In the middle of the farm stood his large mansion, but he was rarely there. Near the house was a runway, where he landed in his plane every few days. He'd circle over his whole plantation and look everything over from the air, then land. He'd climb into a waiting jeep and drive around the farm. He, too, wore those two-dollar trousers and shirt with a cowboy hat and spurs on his Western boots. Whenever he showed up in the fields, most of the Mexicans made themselves scarce.

In one part of his farm, he had forty thousand mature pecan trees. They were so far apart that rows of melons could be planted between them. Now, they were ripe, in late May 1945. They were cantaloupes, which we were supposed to harvest working with the Mexicans, including the four boys. We were allowed to eat as many cantaloupes as we wanted, but too many caused diarrhea. They were as sweet as sugar, and only a certain size was harvested, not yet completely ripe. Any other cantaloupes, whether too large or too small, were just left lying. It was an incredible waste, since we only picked about a third of them.

We collected them in baskets. Mules pulled light two-wheeled carts along the rows, and we loaded the baskets onto the carts, which were then loaded into refrigerator cars filled with crushed ice; we loaded about five or six such cars a day. We wanted to share this unexpected abundance with our fellow POWs in the camp. Every evening before the trip back to camp, we'd fill our water containers with slices of melon and stuff our raincoat sleeves with little cantaloupes. Since it was forbidden to bring anything into camp, and we were frisked by the guards when we returned from work, we'd hang our raincoats over our arms. Raincoats always had to be taken to work. The heavy water cooler had to be lifted up as if it were empty, which was a feat of strength every time. The guards never did guess that we were smuggling cantaloupes into camp. Our fellow POWs were very pleased.

The Land of Enchantment — POW in Las Cruces, New Mexico

Camp life got back to normal again. We had five American movies a week, but the projector was available only on two evenings, so we saw three on one night and two on the other. They were shown outdoors as soon as it got dark. We wrapped up in quilts in front of the screen. When it was a boring movie, we'd nod off. The newsreels showed us what Germany looked like now, and it was depressing.

Our clothing consisted of American uniforms with "PW" stenciled permanently in six-inch-high letters on our shirts and jacket sleeves, as well as on the fronts of our trouser legs and the backs of our overalls. Part of each POW's outfit was a rubberized raincoat that had to be taken to work daily, although we never needed it here. Underwear was turned in for washing and exchanged for clean ones. Anyone who had good clothes washed them himself, though. Things were spread out in the shower with plenty of hot water and soap powder, scrubbed with a brush, then rinsed thoroughly and spread out to dry quickly on the lawn in the sun, no ironing. We only wore white socks, which we exchanged rather than washed.

We still had our German uniforms, which we had taken good care of, but then we were supposed to have "PW" stenciled on them, too, so we didn't ever wear them anymore. In the canteen, there were broad-brimmed Mexican straw hats for sale, and I bought one [see page 125]. But they were impractical for cotton picking, because the brim kept getting stuck in the plants when we bent over.

Under supervision, we also were forced to watch a documentary film about the concentration camps the victors had found in Germany. What had happened there was incomprehensible to us. We had known nothing about them. We could only be ashamed to be Germans.

A Spanish class was offered in camp, and I signed up for it right away. There were only five of us, taught by a Spanish-speaking German POW. We got used textbooks from an elementary school in El Paso, ones used to teach Mexican children English. So we had to learn Spanish through English, which was hard, since Spanish was already difficult enough, plus having to have a foundation in English.

I was able to say simple sentences soon, and naturally, I practiced them with my young friend Junior Barela. This really pleased him, so he told his friends, who all wanted to talk to me now in their native tongue. But I hadn't gotten quite that far yet. One Monday morning, I used my Spanish (after I had carefully constructed the sentence in my head) to ask an old man who could hardly walk, but still had to work to make a living, whether he had gone to the dance the day before. And wonder of wonders, he understood me just fine, but then he laughed and laughed and told everybody what I thought him capable of.

There were still English classes, too, although now there wasn't much interest in them, but I still went regularly. I realized how important it is for people with different languages to be able to speak to each other; I had already benefited from it enormously. A testing board came to our camp to give us an English exam, administered by several American officers. First there were written translations, then an oral test, all of which took about two hours. Those who passed it got a diploma, but it wasn't recognized later in Germany. My friend Ertl, with whom I still spent a lot of time, just didn't want to learn English. He preferred to play sports and got along fine that way.

THE JAPANESE

In early June 1945, we were taken to a Japanese-American farmer named Nakayama, about a half an hour away, toward Hatch. He grew mainly vegetables. We worked fast at his place, which was what he expected of us. When he got into a car or truck, he turned the ignition key before he even closed the door and raced off before he was completely in his seat. When we packed lettuce in crates, working together with his two teenaged daughters, both of them worked incredibly fast. The heads of lettuce seemed to fly, and a crate was full in seconds. We could hardly keep track with our eyes; our pace was more leisurely.

Once, when we were setting out cabbage plants, he let the water from the irrigation ditch flow right behind us to speed us up. We'd finally had enough. We just waved to each other and stopped, but the water kept flowing, and we had to quit. The farmer was mad, because now he would have to wait several days until the soil had dried out again.

So he thought up another system. Every morning, when we started work, he assigned us that day's quota; whenever we were finished, he'd take us back to camp. All of a sudden, we were able to work faster, and we were done by two or three o'clock, and he took us back. On the way home, he almost always stopped at a gas station and bought each of us a little something like ice cream, a candy bar, or a Coke, and we really appreciated it. We liked working for him. He and his family were very friendly; his two pretty daughters with their Oriental eyes liked talking to us.

The Land of Enchantment — POW in Las Cruces, New Mexico

One day the farmer told us his brother had just arrived home from Germany, where he'd been stationed as an officer in the U.S. Army. If we liked, he'd tell us about the situation in Germany. We wanted to hear his impressions, so we stayed after work. The man arrived in uniform and spoke, to our amazement, perfect German. We sat down on the grass, and he stood before us like a teacher as he reported the following. He, a Japanese-American, had studied in Heidelberg. He'd just arrived from Germany, where his unit had been stationed in Stuttgart. He'd been with the occupation forces in Karlsruhe, Heidelberg, Heilbronn, Bietigheim, Ludwigsburg, and Stuttgart, all in southwestern Germany, near my home.

This was just the fellow for me, and everyone had lots of questions. I wanted to know how things looked around my hometown; it seemed possible from where he'd been that he even knew Gross-Sachsenheim. He reported about the destruction of Pforzheim, Heilbronn, and Stuttgart and knew that the viaduct in Bietigheim had been wrecked. There wasn't much to eat, people were listless, and no one knew what was going to happen.

All of the Nazis had disappeared, and a new government would now have to be established by the Americans. There were lots more questions for him, and he seemed happy to answer them and glad to be able to use his German. We were very grateful. We silently set off back to the camp, not having had any idea how bad everything was.

For a long time, no mail had come, and everyone wondered what had happened to his family, and whether they were still alive. Fathers of families in particular wondered this. When would we finally get to go home? I'd been a POW for two years now, gone from home for three. I'd had to spend my youth, like many other men, behind barbed wire, and now we were needed at home.

Once again, we were taken to the Stahmann Farm to pick cotton, toward the end of the harvest, and it was hard to fill our quotas. Fearing punishment, we'd toss a handful of sand into our cotton sacks every once in a while so that we'd reach the required weight. The sacks full of picked cotton were emptied into a trailer after they'd been weighed. The loaded trailers were taken to the cotton gin where giant vacuum suction tubes sucked the cotton into the gin.

Mr. Stahmann happened to come by just as our trailer was being unloaded. He noticed the sand lying on the floor of the trailer and screamed in a rage, "Who loaded this trailer?" Naturally, the answer was:

the POWs. He called us together and started yelling about sabotage (whenever something wasn't in order, it was always immediately sabotage). If he found one more grain of sand, he would have us all thrown into prison. Prison didn't scare us much, since we were already locked up, but we were afraid of our captain.

His American interpreter was named Jung, and he was about our age. One evening when he was visiting the camp leader Kehrer in our barracks, I noticed his Pforzheim accent. I asked him about it, and he said he was originally from Pforzheim and had gone to school there. As the son of Jewish parents, he said he'd managed to escape from Germany, but he didn't want to say anything more than that. He always made an effort to be even-handed, but he did have to translate Captain Williams's orders without comment or contradiction.

Our captain grew more and more brutal. He punished every trivial transgression inhumanely; now we were also criminal prisoners. Inside the camp, he had a special stockade fenced in, ten by ten yards, and he locked up anybody who wasn't working hard enough, in his opinion. For days they'd suffer with nothing to eat or drink, without protection from the blazing sun, or the freezing cold at night—but they survived, although they suffered some physical damage.

The fact that they survived made the captain step up the punishment, so that the next ones were locked up without clothes, just underpants. Now they were completely unprotected. After several days, their sunburned skin was in tatters, their lips were swollen, their faces bloated, and they could hardly see out of their eyes. We had to watch helplessly while their moaning almost drove us mad. When they were finally released, they were broken men, and it took quite a while before they had recovered to some extent. Many didn't recover; they were just taken away, and we never heard what had happened to them.

One POW was locked up like this for an entire week for something trivial, and the camp barber had to shave his head first. He tried to cover his head during the day with his hands against the hot sun, until he finally grew too weak to hold his arms up. He lay motionless day and night, rolled up into a ball in the corner, only indicating by his groans that he was even still alive. The whole time we had to watch his suffering and couldn't help. After a week, he was pardoned, and we stood there ready to help him out of the cage.

The Land of Enchantment — POW in Las Cruces, New Mexico

The captain opened the gate, and we started to enter, but he forbade us to. The man had to be able to come out by himself, or he'd have to stay in there. The prisoner sensed that he was being freed, but he couldn't see anymore. He tried to crawl to the gate on his hands and knees and kept bumping into the gatepost. We called out to him which way to move to get out, and at that point, the captain let us take him out. He was little more than a tiny moaning heap of misery, and we didn't know how to touch his sunburned skin. At first, we carried him to the showers, but the medics thought that wasn't the right thing to do; he needed to be taken to a hospital. Our camp leader negotiated with the captain until he finally gave his permission, since he apparently didn't want to have to deal with a death. He was taken to El Paso, and we never heard anything more of him. A few days later, his belongings were picked up; it would have been a miracle if he had survived.

We could never understand how a human being could be so gruesome. Surely he went to church on Sundays. We hadn't done anything to him, and we couldn't be held responsible for the atrocities in the German concentration camps. The civilian population of Las Cruces never learned how we were tortured, or else they didn't want to know about it. Apparently the idea of "Nazi war criminal" had established itself with them, too. Yet we hadn't gone to war voluntarily, but just like the American soldiers, we had been drafted for military service.

We could expect no help from the farmers, either, since they were only interested in our labor, which they had to pay for; otherwise, we were enemies in their eyes. We rarely heard a friendly word from them, and they never gave us anything. Apart from the Japanese farmer, the farmer from Anthony, and my young friend Junior Barela, I never got a thing. I don't know whether my comrades had better experiences. The farmers themselves normally didn't deal with us at all; they had their people to do that. We got along fine with the other farm workers, especially the Mexicans, since they were in the same situation we were, although they often sang their melancholy, harmonious songs at work.

A delegation from the Swiss Red Cross visited us twice during this time. Since they announced their visit in advance, the camp was in perfect shape. We were photographed while eating, and naturally those meals were especially good. Unfortunately, we couldn't talk with them since they were kept at a distance, and they didn't try to talk to us. Resignedly, we decided that we couldn't expect any help from them. One Austrian POW wouldn't leave it alone. He wrote a letter to the International Red Cross in Geneva, probably realizing that the letter would go through the captain's hands.

The next day, the captain ordered this man to come to him in his office and locked the door behind him. We never heard what happened. After the door was locked, blows could be heard and terrible screams, until it got quiet after a while. A panel truck drove up, and the man was carried out covered with a blanket and driven away. The next day his things were picked up, and we never heard anything more about him, either. A cleaning detail had to clean the office afterward, and they reported that there was blood everywhere, even on the walls.★

Three other POWs had had enough and didn't want to put up with any more. They decided to escape to Mexico, a neutral country. They collected up enough food and drink for the escape. It wasn't difficult to get out of the camp. We all knew that the guards in the watchtowers slept during night duty, and the border was only about thirty miles away.

What follows we learned from one of the guards. One night, they got out of the camp while it was dark and hid somewhere during daylight. The next night, they reached the brightly lit Mexican border and found a good place to get through the barbed wire unnoticed. Now they could breathe a sigh of relief. They walked openly along the southern end of the Rocky Mountains until it grew light again. Then cleaned themselves up and wanted to go into the nearest Mexican village to turn themselves in.

They noticed a group of soldiers coming up the slope toward them and figured, fine, now they could turn themselves in; they were in Mexico, after all. With horror, they discovered suddenly that the soldiers were Americans, and that our captain was with them. They were taken prisoner and learned that their protest, that they were in Mexico, was in vain. It was still the U.S.A.; the border they'd crossed was only a fake border. They'd been observed here, but the real border was a few miles farther south, and even if they had reached it, there was an extradition treaty between the U.S.A. and Mexico.

★ This incident cannot be substantiated. Other former POWs who have been interviewed heard rumors of the incident, but did not see it themselves.

The Land of Enchantment — POW in Las Cruces, New Mexico

Now they were really in the soup. This was a genuine morsel for the captain. All of them marched to the road, where several jeeps were waiting. The captain sat on the hood with a whip in his hand, while the three POWs had to run in front of the jeep. If they didn't run fast enough, he whipped them. They had to run all the way back to the camp like that, but they collapsed in exhaustion along the way. He beat them until they got a second wind. Finally they arrived at the camp gate, crawling on hands and feet. There they collapsed altogether and just lay there. The captain just had them loaded onto a truck and taken away; we never heard anything more of these three again, either. According to the Geneva Convention, prisoners of war are permitted to attempt to escape without being punished, and America was also a signatory to this convention.

Now we were not just counted twice a day, but also every two hours during the night. A guard came into the barracks with a flashlight and looked in every bed; if he weren't certain, he'd pull back the blanket. The night the three men fled, it was soon noticed, and then there was an alarm. Whistles ripped us from our sleep, and everyone had to line up. We were all drowsy and didn't have many clothes on as we formed up outside for roll call. They started counting and found three men missing. For hours, the guards searched the entire camp, in the latrine, the washroom, every single bed was taken apart, and the entire area was combed with searchlights, but to no avail. We could hardly stand up by now; we were freezing in the chilly night. The sun was rising on the horizon when we finally were allowed to go back to bed. Three men were missing; this was definitely a painful experience for our captain.

In the summer of 1945, I was twenty-three years old, when eighty newcomers were brought to the camp. We had to set up bunk beds in the barracks, and Ertl put his above mine. It got cramped in the barracks. Until then, we "Africans" had been amongst ourselves, but the newcomers were from Europe, and from them we learned the full extent of the catastrophe in Germany.

The famous health roll calls continued every month, and the newcomers were surprised by it. The Hitler salute was prohibited, which didn't much matter to us, since we'd rarely used it here anyway.

With apprehension, we thought of the coming cotton harvest. Now, not only our outer garments but also our underwear had to be labeled "PW." A number of German scientists were taken to the base camp at Fort Bliss in El Paso, among them Wernher von Braun, the rocket specialist. However, they weren't put in the POW camp but given quarters in the American army base, all of them in civilian clothing. When German POWs there tried to talk to them, they were given the cold shoulder. The scientists clearly wanted nothing to do with us. They were able to move freely and could go into El Paso in the evening. All POWs were furious at them, since they, who had built German rockets, were free to move around, and we, who had just carried out orders, were locked up.

THE NEXT COTTON HARVEST

In September, cotton picking started again, and although we did more and more, it was never enough for our captain. Finally he set the group quota at 210 pounds per man. As an old hand, I was able to reach that easily, but others couldn't, so some had to work harder to make the average come out right. We got two newcomers in our group, two older men, well fed, with full bellies. One of them had been a regimental chaplain, and the other was an administrator of some kind. Unused to any manual labor at all, they sweated and groaned while picking cotton and picked almost nothing, so everyone else had to work extra hard on their behalf.

One day we also got a bad field with little cotton on the plants, and it was already clear early in the day that we would never make our daily quota. And we didn't, as we returned weak-kneed to camp that evening. The guard, as usual, reported our yield directly to the captain. He did- n't even let us enter the camp but locked us up on the spot. This time it wasn't outside, but in a barred barracks in nothing but our underpants. There were twenty beds, just the frames, but there were forty of us, so it would be two men per bed or sleep on the floor. We weren't told how long we'd be locked up, and naturally there wasn't any dinner, although we were very hungry.

Night came, and it got chilly in the barracks, toward morning really cold; all of us were freezing, and no one could sleep. Morning arrived and the sun rose, and then it got warmer, but by noon it was so hot and humid in the room that we could hardly breathe. It didn't help at all that our bar- racks were right behind the camp kitchen, so that we could continuously smell food cooking, which just made us feel our hunger more acutely. One day followed another, nothing to eat or drink; we got weaker and weaker. We hardly felt the hunger anymore, but the thirst was far worse. Even if we were going to die, none of us felt like he had done anything wrong.

The Land of Enchantment — POW in Las Cruces, New Mexico

On the fifth day, we happened to see our camp leader pass our window, and we called out to him that we were locked up here without cause. We wanted him to go to the captain and ask him to take a look at the cotton field himself. Our camp leader reported to the captain and presented our request to him. And a while later, he actually got in his jeep and drove away; we could only hope for the best. We waited anxiously for his return. Finally, after our long, impatient waiting, he came back. How would this turn out? we wondered. Together with his interpreter, he came to our barracks and told us that if we had exerted ourselves more, we would have been able to make the quota, but he wanted to show mercy, so we were released.

How could this man sleep peacefully in his headquarters on one side of the road, together with the guards, when a scant forty yards away, prisoners were being treated so inhumanely? Obviously, POWs had to work, but maximum output could hardly be expected of them. After all, we wanted to work; none of us ever refused to do so at this camp. After our release, we quickly got dressed again and raced to the mess hall, where the other POWs were at dinner. Although we wanted to start eating, we realized that it wasn't going to be that easy; our throats and stomachs had closed so badly. The kitchen personnel had been watching us and laughing; they were used to this. They brought us tea, which we tried to drink from a spoon, and after a while, we were able to swallow it. But we weren't supposed to eat anything until the tea had opened up our stomachs again. It took days for us to be able to eat normally again, but the next day, we had to go back to picking cotton. Luckily, it was a new field.

Another one of the newcomers to our barracks was Manfred Müller from Westphalia, just sixteen years old. He had been serving as an anti-aircraft volunteer in Italy when he was taken prisoner by the Americans. He was still a child without any whiskers on his pudgy cheeks. He had bright blue eyes and blonde hair. During the day, he wasn't any different than the other POWs, but after lights out at 10:00 PM, he often started to cry, sobbing into his blanket, then sitting up and crying out, "I want to go home, I want to go home." We were unable to console him; he simply wanted to go home to his mother. We were so sorry for him, but there was nothing we could do to help him.

At one point, there was a clothing check, when everything was examined to make sure the "PW" was stenciled on it.

Another year (1945) was drawing to a close, and we were still imprisoned. Franz Ertl had heard nothing from his family in the Sudetenland, although we had heard about brutal mass expulsions. Many of us were worried about their families and relatives. In letters, wives complained that they were unable to take care of things alone, men were sorely needed everywhere, children didn't know their fathers anymore, and here we had to keep slaving away picking cotton.

Our daily output kept rising, but mainly out of fear of punishment. My record for one day was 377 pounds; even native laborers didn't pick more than that. Moreover, it wasn't a very long working day. In the morning we had to wait until the last drop of dew had evaporated, and in the evening, as soon as it started to cool off, we had to stop. Cotton could only be picked when it was completely dry. The drive out to the field often took more than an hour, with the most distant farm being some fifty miles away. On these long trips, we lay down on partially filled cotton sacks in the big trailer trucks. The highway ran straight as an arrow along the railroad line, with small curves only at the stations.

In the autumn, when it started getting dark earlier, it was interesting to look into people's lighted homes as we drove by and to see how they lived, since curtains were unknown here.

We didn't have much of a celebration for Christmas 1945 apart from a small banquet; no one was in a very festive mood. We didn't know when, or even if we would ever be released, given everything we had heard about what had happened during the war. The newspapers were full of German atrocities we were now having to pay for.

By late January 1946, the cotton picking was finished, and we were all glad, because now the workload would decrease somewhat, since there was no quota with our other kinds of work. We were surprised on 1 February 1946 to receive black uniforms for all of us. No one had an explanation for it; perhaps it had something to do with our imminent release? Franz Ertl, with whom I'd been together all this time, was transferred to another camp. There were quite a lot of transfers all of a sudden.

Then, finally, the first signs of our release. We allowed ourselves to hope. At the end of February, lists of names scheduled for release were issued. Everyone was relieved—we were going to get to go home after all. Soon the first trains started leaving from El Paso. Franz Ertl came through our camp briefly on his way home, and we said goodbye for the last time with the promise of seeing each other again someday in Germany.

THE TRIP HOME

And then my name was on the list. I was glad, but then I noticed that all the other names on the list came from the Soviet Occupation Zone (my home was in the American Zone).★ I mentioned this immediately to our camp leader, thinking there was something wrong. He checked it out and said it was true; someone had assumed that Gross-Sachsenheim was located in Saxony in the Soviet Zone, but he'd take care of it right away. Up to that point, no one going to the American Zone had been released, and there was no date given for their release. I told him not to bother. If I could just get back to Germany as quickly as possible, I could figure out how to get home on my own. Whatever you want, he said—and it turned out to be a fateful mistake.

I spent all the money I'd saved up in the canteen on several cans of coffee, cocoa, tea, sugar, sweetener, underwear, sewing materials, towels, and so forth, until my money was all gone. By chance, in those final days we were again working in the field with my Mexican friends. When I told Junior that I was leaving soon and would never see him again, he grew quite sad. The next morning, he brought me a photograph that he had had taken the previous evening; on my last day, I brought him a photo of me in uniform. He was delighted and showed it proudly to all his buddies, and he wanted me to write to him soon. When we shook hands for the last time and I wished him good luck, tears came to his eyes, and he turned away quickly.

It was an indescribable feeling to drive through our camp gate in a truck for the very last time, into freedom, knowing that it would probably be a long journey until I was back in Gross-Sachsenheim.

First we went to the main camp at Fort Bliss, past the fields where we'd invested so much sweat. The Mexicans who waved to us as we drove past, we knew personally. In the main camp, we had to spend a couple of days waiting. A volunteer labor detail was sought, but since I'd always been against volunteering, I didn't sign up. They had to pick up empty shells on the firing range. On the last day before the departure of the volunteers, a

---

★ After World War II, Germany was divided into four occupation zones: American, British, French, and Soviet.

dud exploded when they threw it into a truck. Several men were killed, and others were injured.

Through the aunt of our camp leader Kehrer, the horrible misdeeds of our Captain Williams were made known after our return, and the deaths for which he had been responsible were investigated. He was brought before a court and sentenced, but I never found out what his punishment was. He then died at a relatively early age.★

We were permitted to pack our belongings into two duffle bags each, but together they weren't allowed to weigh more than eighty-five pounds. However, we didn't have a scale, so we had to guess at the weight. Both duffle bags then had to be weighed before we shipped out, and if they were too heavy, the guard just kept taking things out until the weight was acceptable, even if a single shoe was left without its partner. The long journey started on my twenty-fourth birthday, on 19 March 1946. An express train was waiting for us at the military base at Fort Bliss.

Everyone got aboard, three men for each four seats, as before. At 10:00 AM, the train slowly left the base, headed along the Rio Grande, past our familiar fields and through Las Cruces, right past our camp. Other POWs were waiting for our train to pass, and as they waved to us, we cried tears of joy and watched the camp disappear behind us. Our first stop was in Santa Fe, where the locomotive took on water. Then we headed into the Rocky Mountains, where we saw snow again for the first time in a while. It was cold outside, with heaps of snow on each side of the cleared single-spur train tracks. It was a wonderful feeling to travel so quietly through the snow.

But then we went downhill once more into spring-like countryside, via Kansas City on to Chicago. A sea of houses came into view, and I asked our accompanying guard what city this was. He told me excitedly that it was Chicago; we'd be going past his home any minute. Then he pointed out the window and said there was his house; had I seen it? he asked, and I said, of course, even though I wasn't quite sure.

This trip was more pleasant than the westward journey had been. Every returnee was allowed to take one of his five quilts home with him, so we

---

★ There is no evidence available that Captain Williams was court-martialed after World War II. In fact, he served as a counterintelligence officer in Germany after the war. He died in 1992 at the age of eighty-one.

could make ourselves comfortable at night. The guards riding with us paid little attention to us except to ask for an occasional cigarette.

Many of us could now talk to them in their language. The trip took three and a half days until the evening we reached Camp Shanks, twenty miles from New York City. Most of the returnees knew this giant camp, where POWs from all over America arrived to be assembled for transport back to Europe by ship.

We were again assigned barracks and bunk beds in the usual arrangement. Meals were served in a giant mess hall, since there were thousands of POWs in the camp; it was very efficient. The first group took the first table, the next group the next table, and so on until the last table was taken, and by then, the first table was free again. I was in this camp for six days with nothing to do but eat and take walks.

One evening I happened to meet my friend Georg Schröder, who had disappeared without a trace near Beja in Tunisia; we had a lot to tell each other. There was a high rate of suicide in this camp. Apparently some men were afraid of going home. We never knew quite why, whether they'd done something to be ashamed of or had family problems. Here too, there were roll calls twice daily, lining up by barracks on the broad camp street. One time a man was missing from our barracks; we found him hanging from a rafter in the barracks, already dead.

Our last meal in this camp, in fact our very last meal in America, was pork chops with mashed potatoes and cabbage. Our time was finally up, and we could leave.

Again aboard the train, we raced along the curving tracks along the Hudson River to New York City, bouncing from side to side. From the terminal, we descended a spiral staircase to the pier and were taken by small ferryboat to our ship, which had anchored in the harbor and was almost fully loaded. The ship was the *Aiken,* a twelve-thousand-ton troop transport converted from a freighter. In what had been the holds there were five levels of bunks and very narrow passageways; we could hardly move, it was so full.

FAREWELL, AMERICA

We were apparently the very last ones aboard; they'd been waiting just for us to get under way. This may have been the reason for the breakneck train trip. It was nighttime, and as soon as we were all on board, the ship sailed.

Very slowly, we left the harbor, but because we were called to supper, we couldn't say goodbye to the Statue of Liberty. We were tired and soon went to bed in the narrow bunks. I had the lowest one; whenever anyone in one of the upper bunks wanted to climb down, he had to step on my bed frame, which woke me up every time. Our pairs of duffle bags also took up a lot of room.

The next morning, we were already on the open ocean beyond sight of land. We could go up on deck whenever we liked. There were washrooms and toilets on board, and we stood in line to get our meals; the mess hall was also crowded. For the first few days, it was a nice voyage, and we were all in a good mood—we were headed home. But then came stormy weather, and the ship wallowed in the waves, up and down, and our stomachs rebelled. The first seasick men started throwing up.

As long as I could, I stayed on deck. It was impressive to watch the waves grow higher and higher as the sea raged and the wind howled around the superstructure. But when the waves started coming over the rails, everyone had to leave the decks and the hatches were closed. Outside in the fresh air, I hadn't felt sick, but once I went below into the stuffy air, I felt an irrepressible urge to throw up. I lay down in my bunk, and I felt a little better; I was still nauseous, but I no longer felt like I had to vomit. So I just stayed lying down for the next few days and didn't dare think of eating. Wherever I turned, I could hear the groans of seasick, vomiting comrades; that pretty well finished me off. Almost no one was eating anymore. Fortunately, one of the big ventilation pipes to the deck was opened, and plenty of fresh air blew into the hold. It was quite cold, but the fresh air felt good to all of us.

After three days, the sea grew calmer, although the ship still rocked up and down for quite a while. Then on the fourth day, the yawing stopped, and we were allowed to go back up on deck; food tasted good again, we felt better, our good mood returned, and soon we would be home.

Suddenly the pounding and vibrations of the ship stopped, and we didn't know what was wrong. The ship stopped in mid-Atlantic, with waves breaking against the sides and the wind howling over the decks. We grew restless and wondered what was going on. But then, three hours later, we got under way again, and we breathed a sigh of relief. All returnees were called up to the steward's office, where we got back the papers and money that had been confiscated from us at Sidi-Bel-Abbés in Algeria, still in the same envelopes. I got back my 2,950 Tunisian francs, but they probably weren't worth anything now.

The voyage went on and on, with everyone up on deck despite the chill. On the tenth day, we sighted land and entered the English Channel; the ship went slower and slower. In the distance, we could hear bells ringing across the water, and then we saw wrecks in the water, sometimes just the tip of a masthead, sometimes a whole stern section or bow sticking out of the water. Then we heard bells again; every wreck was marked with a bell-buoy. It was ghostly to move between so many sunken ships, in which there must have been many dead men.

At the entrance to the Scheldt River, at the port of Antwerp, Belgium, the ship stopped completely. Now we could see the land more clearly. Our first impression of Europe was devastating. Everywhere we looked there were blasted trees and black stumps sticking up, with destroyed and burned-out houses, and not a soul to be seen. On top of everything else, there was an eerie stillness. The vibrating ceased as the ship's engines stopped. We had to await the flood tide. In America, we hadn't seen or sensed the war; everything there took its normal peacetime course. Here, we were again confronted with the war, even if the cannons were silent. It was cold in Europe.

———

CHAPTER FOUR

Instead of Repatriation, to Labor Camps in England, April 1946–July 1947

INTRODUCTION

*W*alter and his comrades, who expected to return home, hoped
that their ship would land in Germany. Instead, they arrived
in Antwerp, Belgium, from whence they were transported
by train to Brussels and marched to a British-controlled POW camp outside of Brussels. Walter was perplexed when the British provided him
with a new registration number, particularly since the POWs expected
to be released in a few days. Their British camp commander promised
them repatriation, but only after they dismantled the fence around their
camp. Transported back to Antwerp, his group was put on small ferries,
and instead of sailing to Hamburg, they landed in London. The British
informed them over loudspeakers that instead of being discharged, they

77

would have to work in the reconstruction of England, which had been bombed by the Germans.

Walter was devastated after finding out that his captivity would be extended. Instead of being reunited with their families, Walter's unit arrived in Manchester after a thirteen-hour train ride, where the British marched them to a dilapidated camp. Adding to the misery, the English soldiers confiscated almost everything Walter had purchased in the United States and had brought along in two large duffle bags. We can sympathize with Walter, when he mentions that he and his comrades were completely distraught about their fate, and states that "anyone who had believed in a good and just God now had his doubts."

Why did the United States delay repatriation of a large number of its German POWs after Nazi Germany's capitulation on 8 May 1945? The 1929 Geneva Convention stipulated that repatriation of prisoners had to be executed "with the least possible delay after the conclusion of the peace." Though hostilities in Europe had officially ended in May 1945 with the Wehrmacht's acceptance of Germany's unconditional surrender, the United States and Germany had not signed a peace treaty. Thus, the United States had an excuse to postpone repatriation of its German POWs. Those POWs not directly released to Germany were assigned for the reconstruction of industries and agriculture in Allied European countries.

The transfer of POWs from the United States to Great Britain goes back to an agreement reached by the two countries in January 1943 on the basis of which the United States agreed to keep those POWs who originally were to be transferred to Britain. The British government had argued that it could not accommodate large numbers of POWs in their country during wartime. When the United States started shipping back German POWs in 1945, the British claimed their contingent of prisoners from the United States, whom they would transport to labor camps. Consequently, the United States turned over to Britain about 123,000 German prisoners who had been held in American POW camps.

A similar agreement was reached with the French, who received about 55,000 German POWs from U.S. camps. Thus, of the 378,898 German POWs in the United States, about 178,000, or 47 percent, had to work in the reconstruction of war-damaged industries and agriculture in Britain, France, and other European countries, instead of being immediately repatriated to Germany. In fact, the United States transferred about 700,000

Instead of Repatriation, to Labor Camps in England

POWs to France, 175,000 to Great Britain, 30,000 to Belgium, and 50,000 to other countries in Europe from their POW camps in both the United States and Europe.

Quite naturally, the German POWs resented their prolonged captivity in Europe. Many of them, including Walter, considered their extended postwar captivity a punitive measure imposed by the Allies. Though conditions were less than ideal for many POWs, particularly in France, most of those working in Britain fared considerably better than those POWs who were in Soviet captivity, many of whom were not released until 1955, ten years after the end of the war.

At the end of July 1946, the last German POWs were shipped back from the United States to Europe, and by June 1947, the U.S. Army in Europe released its last prisoners held on European soil. Thus, the United States was the first Allied country to return its POWs. Finally, due to domestic pressure in the United States, the U.S. government in 1947 urged the French government to release their German POWs, of whom more than 440,000 were still working in France at that time.

Despite the unwanted extension of his captivity, Walter's stay in London was fairly enjoyable and full of adventures. One of his employers, who elevated him to foreman of a small POW group, was supposedly the Secretary-General of the British Labour Party, who was close to Foreign Secretary Ernest Bevin and Prime Minister Clement Attlee. Walter also befriended a family who originally had lived in the vicinity of Walter's home in Germany and had immigrated to Britain before the outbreak of World War II. He got acquainted with a British female officer, who even wanted to marry him and with whom he corresponded long after his return to Germany. Due to his knowledge of the English language, which he had acquired by having enrolled in English language courses in American POW camps, Walter was able to establish many valuable contacts with British civilians.

He records how the British gradually provided their POWs more freedom. In contrast to France, where some German POWs after the war were harshly treated, the British dealt with their prisoners in a fair and correct manner. Life and work for Walter were not only tolerable, but also at times exciting. Nevertheless, the desire to return to his home country as soon as possible was strong. Having spent more than a year in England as a POW, Walter finally learned at the end of May 1947 that he was to be released.

After being shipped to northern Germany, Walter's unit was transported to a big camp near Münster. There, he met POWs who had just come from Russia. Seeing these men with "nothing but skin and bones, with swollen heads, dressed in rags," Walter realized how fortunate he had been despite some bad experiences. With few exceptions, the American and British armies had fed their POWs well, had provided good medical care and recreational facilities, and given them the opportunity to further their education.

Walter finally received his discharge papers in Dachau. After seeing this "notorious concentration camp," Walter posed the question: "How had human beings been able to stand this for years?"

His journey home on overcrowded trains through ruined cities and bombed-out villages and towns was depressing, especially since he had left his country as a young soldier in 1942, four and a half years earlier. But unlike many other POWs whose families had been killed or had been forced to leave their homes, Walter found his parents and his girlfriend still alive in the little town of Gross-Sachsenheim. He now could start a new life.

— WOLFGANG T. SCHLAUCH

After two hours, the ship started up again, the engine vibrated, and we slowly got under way, moving almost soundlessly into the Scheldt, which is several miles wide at its mouth. It was a Sunday morning, and for the first time we could hear church bells again. In the hazy distance we could make out the steeple of Antwerp Cathedral. Behind a broad dike, the land was considerably below sea level; from our high shipboard vantage point, we could look down the chimneys of the houses. We drew nearer to the city of Antwerp. At 12:00 noon, we tied up at the pier. Everyone disembarked, and a long passenger train was waiting there for us. We had actually hoped to land in Germany, and now here we were in Belgium. The train departed and traveled along curving tracks through the city. It was snowing lightly, and the city looked as if it were dusted with powdered sugar, all looking very quaint after the great expanses of America.

In a station outside Brussels the train stopped and we all got out. It was very cold, and we were shivering in our light clothing. I picked up my baggage, one duffle sack on my shoulder, the other under my arm, and started walking in a long line along a narrow path up a hill. Our load got heavier and heavier, and we were gasping for breath, but there was no break; we

Instead of Repatriation, to Labor Camps in England

were driven on by British soldiers. Why British soldiers, we wondered to ourselves, when we were American POWs? The duffle bags got heavier and heavier, and they were awkward to carry. We had all worked up a sweat, and the road seemed endless.

Suddenly I heard a familiar voice behind me, and when I turned to see who it was, I saw my old friend Franz Ertl, who had left two weeks before me. This was a strange surprise. He told me that they hadn't taken a train to New York, but to the West Coast, where they had taken a ship the long way around through the Panama Canal to New York, where I had embarked. In the crowded confusion aboard ship, we hadn't bumped into each other, but now we were together again.

Finally, we came to a British camp on top of the hill, which also made us wonder what was going on; we wanted to go home, not into another camp. The camp was quite large but very primitive. Our lodging was meant for twelve men; it was a three-foot-deep ditch with a bare-earth floor and a canvas roof over it. This was where we were supposed to sleep, although it was cold, with snow lying everywhere. Luckily, we still had our quilts from America with us. Otherwise we would have frozen to death, since we weren't used to cold weather anymore, either in Africa or in the American Southwest, where it was hot everywhere.

Only the hope of going home soon made things bearable. Luckily, we had all taken coats with us, so with clothes, coats, and quilts, we managed to survive the cold fairly well. The food was poor, a thin stew, but at least it was warm.

Outdoors, we could wash in cold water, but most men didn't bother. The latrine was just a log over a ditch, quite a come-down for us spoiled POWs, but it was only going to last for a couple of days. The camp was again divided up into barbed-wire enclaves with an open space of about thirty yards between the individual enclosures.

The next morning, we couldn't believe our eyes. In the next enclosure across the no-man's-land, girls and young women were crowded up against the fence looking curiously over at us. But the way they looked! They seemed totally neglected with chopped-off hair, uncombed; they regarded us with sad eyes. We shouted across the fence to ask who they were. The answer: they had been army auxiliary girls, what we in Germany had called *Blitzmädel* (female signal corps), who had been captured and locked up here. All their things had been confiscated, and now they had no soap, combs, lotions, nothing. They couldn't even bathe or mend their clothes.

This was real meanness on the part of the victors, and we simply had to do something to help. We had enough with us, which we'd actually meant to take home. Everyone contributed something, and we threw it over to the girls. If it was too light, we tied a stone to it, and almost everything reached its target. They eagerly picked up everything and went away, one after the other, until they were all gone. After a while, the first ones started to come back, and what a transformation we saw! The Cinderellas had turned into pretty girls. They thanked us profusely, and we were glad to have been able to help them; some assistance had really been needed. But with their monthly needs, we couldn't help; we simply hadn't thought of that.

After a week in this inhospitable camp, we got back on a train and were taken to another camp, near Berchem not far from the French border, but still in Belgium. When we arrived, we were all once more registered and assigned new numbers; mine was AA013120. We found that silly for the few days we'd be here, since we were about to be released. We were allowed to write a postcard home, to let them know we were on our way.

The food here was even worse. A cup of tea and some cookies in the morning and at night, with a thin soup at noon; we grew ever more miserable. We were housed in barracks, at least, but they couldn't be heated, so we were still freezing. Snow still lay on the ground, and a cold wind blew through the camp.

After a few days, the English commandant had us assemble and spoke to us in German: You will be released shortly, but beforehand, you will help us dismantle the fences around the camp, since it's being closed down. Anyone who wants to run away can do so; good luck to him. Otherwise, it's possible that those of you traveling to the Soviet Zone (apart from me, everyone in our group came from the Soviet Zone) who get picked up by the French or the Russians may end up not seeing home for quite a while. So, he advised, it would be better to stay here for a few days and get released with official identification papers. If everyone helps, the fence can be dismantled in two days, and British soldiers will help you.

Some of us complained, but no one took off. And two days later, the fence was gone. It was a real chore, since we didn't have any gloves or warm work clothes, and we were hungry, too.

Instead of Repatriation, to Labor Camps in England

A column of British trucks came into the camp. We climbed aboard and traveled across Belgium via Brussels, and returned to Antwerp. We were baffled and asked the officers why we were going this way, and why we couldn't just return directly to Germany. An officer answered that all the Rhine bridges had been destroyed, and we were going to be taken by ship to Hamburg. Well, another day or so didn't matter.

Around midnight, we were loaded onto small ferries outfitted only with benches. Crowded together, we sat there as the ship left the harbor. The wind came up while we were still in the Scheldt estuary, then became a regular storm, and the little ship was thrown around. The first men got seasick and ran to the toilet, and then more and more got sick. Everyone tried to get to the toilets, but they were already occupied by men throwing up. Many just couldn't hold it any longer and threw up wherever they were standing; only a few made it to the railing. It stank terribly everywhere. Seasickness is really terrible, and one simply wants to die; I know from firsthand experience.

When it grew light, the sea calmed down, and we could breathe easier. And then the captain ordered us to clean up the ship. Weakened and feeling miserable, we cleaned up the mess. The sun rose, and some of us realized that we weren't headed for Hamburg. They were comforted and told those were sandbanks we had to sail around. We didn't see any sandbanks, and then an announcement came over the PA system to come on deck. We lined up in a semicircle and found ourselves surrounded by soldiers with machine guns, the safety off. No one had any clue what was now going on. Then came a voice over the PA, in German: "Now hear this: You are not being released. You are needed for reconstruction work in England. We will be landing in London in one hour."

There was a deathly stillness. That just couldn't be true. Surely they were joking. But we saw the armed guards. The quiet lasted a few moments longer, then the complaints started in earnest. They can't be doing this to us; those pious Englishmen can't possibly have deceived us like this. Everyone felt terrible, and many broke into tears. Especially older fathers of families just couldn't hold it back, and the younger men were desperate, too. How many more blows of fate were we going to have to bear? I'd already been away from home for four years, three of those as a POW—wasn't that enough?

Resistance would have been futile against the soldiers, but what about those at home expecting us? The sun was shining brightly when we landed in London. Everyone had to disembark quickly or get a rifle butt in the small of his back. Franz Ertl got a blow that hurt for hours. Double time with our baggage, which had gotten a bit lighter in Belgium. Into a station hall, drink a waiting cup of tea on the run, hand back the cup. A passenger train was waiting for us on the platform, and everyone had to hurry up and get aboard, then off we went. We'd had nothing to eat on board ship, and here we'd only gotten a cup of tea without milk or sugar. From all the throwing up on the ship, our stomachs were really empty.

The trip to the north of England in upholstered seats showed us the country from its most lovely side. Here it was already spring, with shining green, hilly meadows, everything blooming, constant change between sunshine and dark clouds, herds of cattle grazing, everything looking so peaceful. But we were infuriated and swore never to forget this.

After a thirteen-hour trip, we arrived in Manchester, where we got off the train on a sidetrack and made a short march through the city. We realized that the people were taking no notice of us whatsoever; they seemed used to German POWs. The camp we came to was an abandoned yarn-spinning factory several stories high, an old brick building with low ceilings, so that a tall man could just barely stand erect. These ceilings would have been just about right for child labor in the old days, but for us it was oppressively claustrophobic.

First we were searched again and had to lay everything on a table, including the clothes we were wearing. English soldiers greedily grabbed our quilts, then everything we'd brought from America. Of the contents of the two duffle bags, only a miserably tiny amount remained. We then received English uniforms dyed black with a square cut out of the back and pants legs, which had been replaced with a square of different-colored fabric. With this came scratchy underwear, collarless shirts, a denim coverall for work, and shoes with thick rubber soles. We were now completely devastated; anyone who had believed in a good and just God now had his doubts.

As we drew nearer to the camp, one older man got quite excited and said he recognized this camp—he'd been imprisoned here during World War I. When we regarded him skeptically, he said, just wait, my name will be in the stairwell, where I scratched it way back then. And it was true; nothing had changed in this camp since then. Later, my uncle Karl Schelling from Bissingen told me that he, too, had been in that same camp in the First World War. On the street side, where there was heavy traffic, there was a high barbed-wire fence. Its lower strands had already rusted away and been replaced by new wire.

The back of the factory was bordered by a canal, which had earlier furnished water for the machinery. In the big, empty machine halls, we were housed in iron bunk beds without mattresses, just blankets. At night, the hall was locked from outside, and buckets were placed in the corner as toilets; near them, it stank horribly. We spent thirteen days here without working, interrupted only once by a common shower. Over a thousand men lined up; the first hundred stripped and stood under a sprinkler system with a hundred showerheads. When they were ready, the water was turned on. It came lukewarm out of the showerheads, and we were hardly wet when it stopped again. Everybody soaped up, then a brief spray of water, barely enough to rinse off, done, and then the next hundred men.

After that, we had to walk with our arms raised past an officer who was looking for members of the SS, who had their blood group tattooed on their underarms. Since we had been examined so often, he didn't find any. Admittedly, many SS men tried to remove this tattoo by cutting it out with a razor blade or burning it off, but a scar always remained and gave them away.

On 25 May 1946, we were lined up in alphabetical order, and I was again separated from my friend Ertl. Again, we marched through the city. This time, we had light baggage, only the sorry remainder they'd left us, as we walked to the station and took the train back to London. Again we regarded the peaceful countryside, each of us alone with his thoughts. Just a few days earlier, our homes had seemed so close, and now once more so far away; and we had no idea what awaited us now.

Baker Street Station in London was our destination. We got out of the train and climbed into waiting trucks. We drove through the city but didn't see much, since the trucks had canvas covers. We ended up in Osterley Park in the west of London, a park with big, old trees, surrounded by a high brick wall. Between the trees stood barracks, into which four hundred of us moved. They had cement floors and were empty except for iron bunk beds with thin mattresses and rough blankets. The latrine was outside on a porch; under the toilet seats were tin buckets. When they were full, they were taken to a remote corner, poured in a large pan, covered with gasoline, and set afire. The washrooms and showers were good, always with enough warm water at our disposal.

The English camp commandant was an older captain, a calm, almost amiable, plump little man with a typical mustache. He picked out a good-looking young fellow from our ranks to serve as his aide and all-around servant, from whom we then learned all the news of the camp and our imprisonment. During the war, this camp had been used by English soldiers who had manned anti-aircraft guns against German planes.

VICTORY CELEBRATION

Toward the end of 1946, a big victory celebration was planned in London. All the Allies who had participated in the war against us were supposed to take part, and a huge tent city was built for them in London's Hyde Park. This was our first work detail. We were brought in trucks to lay wooden boardwalks between the tents so that the residents could move around with dry feet even in wet weather. Mainly soldiers from overseas were billeted here, East Indians, colored men, blacks, a colorful mixture. We did this work together with British soldiers. I had the advantage of being able to speak English reasonably well, although this English was different from American English.

We weren't able to see the victory parade, just the aircraft as they roared over us with their colored contrails, and artillery could be heard. The victory celebration was on a Saturday. The following Monday, we were brought back to Hyde Park to dismantle everything. The tents were empty, and all the delegates had headed home. They left a lot behind, or had forgotten it; we found our first English coins under the boardwalk. In one of the kitchen tents stood several large cans with powdered milk, sugar, cocoa, and lemon powder. We didn't want to take them without asking. I found one of the chefs and asked him; he laughed and said, of course, we could take all of it. In the camp, we stirred a mixture of all these ingredients, heated it up, and poured it into mess tins to cool; it made pretty good chocolate.

And we got to know Hyde Park and the nearby Kensington Gardens. This was a huge park right in the middle of London with trees from all over the world, deep green lawns, more like a meadow, where everyone could spend time without any "Keep Off the Grass" signs. There were lakes with swans and ducks, the famous water gardens, and the Royal Albert Memorial. It was a paradise for children, too. After three weeks, our work was done, and the park was cleared.

A CHANGE OF CAMPS

We left the Osterley Park camp and were transferred to another London suburb, Enfield, in Bullsmoor Lane. Again wooden barracks, in the midst of a residential community. This time it wasn't barbed wire, but chicken wire, and no watchtowers. Thirty men to a barracks, wooden bunk beds, a coal stove in the middle. In the washing barracks, there were even bathtubs in addition to individual showers. Another surprise was the toilet barracks, with lockable toilet stalls, but no urinals for the men. Everything seemed rather strange. Guards explained it to us: this had been a camp for female personnel in the British army, serving in London. In Germany, we had called them *Blitzmädel* (female signal corps).

Our English camp commandant came with us, together with his German aide. Of course, we weren't here for a vacation. Work groups were assigned, and everyone got a work number; mine was 455. The very next morning, trucks showed up to take the work details to their various jobs. In a detail of twelve, I was taken into central London, to Whitehall, the government quarter. We had to get out at No. 9, Trafalgar Square, where we were taken up to the third floor. In an empty room, we were told to wait, and our driver disappeared. There we sat, alone, not knowing one another, and waited. After a while, the door opened, and an elderly gentleman in civilian clothes, with gray hair, a prominent nose, and protruding teeth, came into the room, slightly bent over. He looked all of us over, and then asked in English which of us spoke English. No one seemed to understand. Although I did, in fact, understand, I didn't say anything; maybe someone understood better than I did. The gentleman asked again, and no one spoke up. Finally, I came forward. He shook my hand and introduced himself as Handford and asked my name. On the spot, he made me his interpreter and adjutant. An interesting time was about to start for me.

LONDON

He explained our task to me: during the war, many wealthy English families had moved out to their country estates because of the German bombing raids. Their elegant London homes were empty, so the British government had requisitioned these houses and occupied them with English female soldiers who were on duty in London as drivers, switchboard operators, etc. Now that the war had been over for more than a year, these families wanted their London homes back. Our mission was to empty these houses; many of the young women were discharged, and those remaining were grouped together, and we were also supposed to help them move. When I translated this for my fellow POWs, they were excited; this was a job more to their liking, since they were all in their early twenties.

We were picked up in a truck, with our boss, Mr. Handford, sitting up front and us in the back, and off we went. After a short trip within London, we stopped in front of a magnificent mansion. We were supposed to load beds, wardrobes, tables, and chairs. I wanted to join in, but the boss stopped me, reminding me that I was his adjutant, and not supposed to do manual labor. As a sign of my elevated status he took a white armband out of his pocket and pulled it over my sleeve; I was supposed to have it on at all times. While the others worked at a leisurely pace, he and I talked, often for hours. It turned out that he was a well-known man in England, a city councillor in London and Secretary-General of the Labour Party who held several other positions. Since he was now elderly, he had taken on the assignment for the government of preparing these homes to be returned to their owners. During his term of office, he had often been in delegations visiting Hitler and Stalin; he must have been quite an important man. One of his school friends was the Foreign Secretary at that time, Bevin, and he met Prime Minister Attlee once a week. He was still a very accomplished public speaker, and he told me quite a lot about these weekly discussions, and also said that he often conveyed my opinions to his friends.

The house had been emptied in the meantime, so we all got back in the truck, sitting comfortably in the chairs we were moving, and off we went right through the middle of London. The weather was good and the sun was shining as we drove over Tower Bridge headed south, toward the slums of London, where the poor lived. We left London and turned off after an hour into a park where there were large warehouses; here we unloaded our freight. Until 1936, the reconstructed Crystal Palace had stood here, where great concerts had taken place; even Handel was said (erroneously) to have played here. The palace had collapsed, and only the foundation was still standing, with broken glass and bent iron beams everywhere. It was rumored that the Crystal Palace had been destroyed on purpose and in advance so that German bombers could not find their way by its reflection. I doubted that, since they would have otherwise removed all the broken panes of glass. I later learned that it had, in fact, been destroyed by fire in 1936.

Instead of Repatriation, to Labor Camps in England

Our driver, a young man on military duty, came from the north of England and didn't yet know his way around London, so our boss had to give him directions. By now it was noon, so we took a break in the great empty hall and ate our lunch. Next door was also a toilet, so that problem had been solved. The boss and the driver left and didn't come back until after lunch. We drove up to another elegant home, with the girls still living in it. They just had to move together into an annex. We were glad to help them carry their belongings and mattresses, and although my crew spoke no English, they got along fine right away. It was a lot of fun for all of us. So that we wouldn't get finished in one day, my men took their time with the job in order to have to come back the next day, to the girls' delight. We were all quite young and well groomed, freshly shaven, with good haircuts. Only the dark brown uniforms with the patches were out of place; otherwise we made a good impression on the girls. Sadly, after we had gotten to know each other a bit, we had to be on our way again.

England is known for its tea drinkers; they need a "cuppa" every couple of hours. We, too, were supposed to be turned into tea drinkers. There wasn't much point in taking hot tea with us to work, since it would be cold by noon. So the next day, I went into the girls' kitchen and asked their chef for hot water for the tea I'd brought along. She brewed my tea for me in a big pot and asked whether we wanted milk and sugar. We prisoners didn't get things like that, I told her, and she responded that one couldn't drink tea without milk and sugar, so she generously gave me both.

Then I asked her if there were anything left over from their lunch, and if so, could we have it before it was thrown away, since my young men were always hungry. That must have gotten around among the girls, because after we'd had our usual lunch in the empty hall, they brought us plates of meat, salad, noodles, and even pudding for dessert. The girls had obviously heard about my request and had eaten almost nothing so that plenty would be left over for us. We were moved and ate like famished day laborers, leaving nothing on the plates. The girls stayed there watching us and were glad we were enjoying the food. The weeks passed with some surprise almost every day; we always found some little place where we got something to eat. At every new job site, I had my little routine ready: if there's something left over, etc. We were frequently invited to dinner: when we were in the neighborhood, we should drop in. We took them at their word.

After six weeks, Mr. Handford said, "Walter, you know your way around London well enough now. From now on, you can manage by yourself. It's getting to be too much for me. You'll get instructions every morning on what is to be done." Every morning we left camp at 7:00 AM and arrived an hour later in Whitehall, where the driver let us off. We went to house No. 9, which belonged to the neighboring War Office, up the stairs to the third floor, after we had greeted the aged lift operator with "Good morning." That always pleased him. In the rooms assigned to us, we waited until 9:00 AM, when the men and our boss arrived at their offices. A soldier took me into the office for my briefing, through long halls. The men were already waiting for me. After a brief greeting, I was asked to sit down and was then told what all there was to do that day, with the addresses written down on a slip of paper. After everything had been explained, I was sent off.

Now we went down to the sidewalk and waited for our truck to arrive. Then the men came downstairs, since they couldn't all wait on the sidewalk, and now our work could begin. The drivers weren't much concerned about our jobs; they were merely responsible for transportation. But we soon had a good relationship with each of our three drivers. The route was discussed, based on the destination we had located on our city map. Whenever we were able to eat with the girls, the driver joined us. Thus he saved a lunch. Since the boss no longer came along, I sat up front and had things a bit more comfortable than my crew, but they had arranged things pretty well in the back of the truck with cushions and rain gear.

I had a number of interesting experiences during this period, but we still wanted to get home at last and be free. We were somewhat freer here, to be sure, without a guard accompanying us, and we could do our jobs the way we wanted to, but it still wasn't complete freedom.

Christmas 1946 approached. At one morning's briefing, an officer told me that all prisoners would be released for Christmas; this was a government decision. I couldn't believe it; we would have to have seen some of the preparations for it by now. I shared my doubts with them, saying we had been lied to so often by the British authorities. They made a £10 bet with me, and I had to go along with it. That wasn't hard, because if we'd actually been released, I wouldn't have been able to pay off the bet. On the first workday after Christmas, I held out my hand when I showed up for briefing. They laughed and took up a collection and gave me the

£10, although they knew quite well that POWs were not allowed to have English money.

THE INVITATION

Right before Christmas of 1946, a call went out to the English population that they could invite German POWs home for Christmas. We received six invitations for four hundred men and decided in the office only to send POWs who could speak English. I was one of those who were assigned a family. On Christmas Day, I was called to the office, where an Englishman, Mr. Gattung, was waiting for me with his ten-year-old son Eric. We were introduced to each other. The camp commandant reminded them not to help me escape and reminded me not to use this as an opportunity to flee. Both of us signed a document to this effect, and then we were free to go. The son kept looking at me out of the corner of his eye. He apparently was nervous about walking next to such a dangerous Nazi war criminal. We were conversing in English, but then Mr. Gattung suddenly said we could speak German, too. Startled, I asked him whether he had been a German POW. No, no, he said, but then he wanted to know where I was from. Not far from Stuttgart, I answered. He was very interested and wanted to know where, exactly. When I said Gross-Sachsenheim, he laughed. I wanted to know whether he happened to know the town. But he didn't answer me. In the meantime, we'd reached his house. His wife was standing in the door. Mr. Gattung said to her, "This is Herr Schmid from Gross-Sachsenheim." She cried out in Swabian dialect, "Whaaat? From Gross-Sachsene? Well, now, if that isn't a surprise, just come right on in. I'll bet he knows what I'm cooking for dinner—a roast with salad and Swabian noodles *(Spätzle)*." I was thoroughly amazed—both of them spoke Swabian dialect, though they were English, and they knew Swabian cooking. Quite bewildered, I asked what was going on. Mrs. Gattung said, "I'm from Ludwigsburg," and then he said, "I'm from Ossweil." We were all surprised now—what a coincidence, when you considered that I was the only POW in the whole camp from the American Zone; all of my fellow POWs were from the Soviet Zone.

It turned out to be a wonderful Christmas for me. Since the children, ten-year-old Eric and his fourteen-year-old sister Margaret, didn't speak German, however, we spoke mostly in English. The children avoided coming too near me, since they, of course, had been taught in school to be against the Germans as enemies. There was a real Swabian noonday meal, but then the obligatory English plum pudding for dessert, drenched with 100-proof rum and lighted. In the afternoon, there were presents, even one for me: handkerchiefs, good soap, and cologne. At first, I felt uncomfortable in this strange setting. The rooms were so small, compared with our familiar barracks, and then sitting in stuffed chairs, with people all dressed up, a beautifully decorated Christmas tree, gifts, everyone so friendly. Everything was so new to me, and there I sat in a POW uniform without any presents to give anyone.

Then it was time to tell our stories, more exciting than any novel. Mrs. Gattung's father, a German from Ludwigsburg, had been imprisoned as a POW in England in World War I and had married an Englishwoman. After that war, times were very hard in England, with many people out of work. So he decided to go back to Germany with his family. One son and one daughter (Mrs. Gattung herself, ten years old at the time) couldn't speak a word of German, but they had to go to a German school in Ludwigsburg, although she hardly fit in a grade-school desk chair. So she grew up in Ludwigsburg and learned normal German. Later she met Herr Gattung from Ossweil, who came from a similar family. In 1937, they had married in the garrison church in Ludwigsburg. Shortly thereafter, they emigrated, together with her brother, to England. Herr, now Mr. Gattung, had learned the trade of goldsmith with Gössele, the watchmaker, in Ludwigsburg, but in England he found no work in this trade. So he became a sales clerk in a butcher shop that made mainly German sausage. So that his children would not have any disadvantages in school, they spoke only English from then on.

Mrs. Gattung's brother, who also lived in London, told his own incredible story. In England, when the war began, he was drafted into the British army. In Greece, he was captured by the Germans and taken as a POW to a farm in Austria, which had an inn. In the evening, he sat with the guests in the inn. Because he was a good accordion player, the farmer got an instrument for him, and he provided the atmosphere in the inn, since he did know all the German songs. After a while, people hardly knew he was only a British POW. It was the best time of his life, he confided to me. His parents in Ludwigsburg received a visit from an important official who wanted to talk them into getting their son into the German army. From the government, they even got travel money to Austria and the guarantee that they could bring their son home immediately. He would get four weeks of leave, and then have to report for duty in the German army. But he wouldn't go along with that, and his parents sadly went home again. He no longer believed the Germans would win the war, he assured me.

Soon thereafter, he was transferred to Eastern Austria. Again, it was a farm, whose owner had been drafted into the German *Wehrmacht*. As the Russian front got closer and closer, he decided to take the farmer's family with him and flee to the West. They took their basic belongings in a farm wagon, and with the reins of the horses in his hand, off they set toward the West. The Russians got ever closer. In one village the Americans had already reached, they got caught by the Russians at a crossing. When they pulled him off the wagon, he tore off his peasant jacket, and there he stood in a British uniform. The Russians didn't recognize the uniform and thought he was in some special German unit. They wanted to beat him to death. In despair, he cried out to the Americans on the other side of the road to come over to him. An American officer ran over, and he explained everything to him.

The American translated this for the Russians, and in the twinkling of an eye, they were completely transformed, hugging him, Russian women kissing him, dancing for joy with him, drinking vodka together. Then, however, he accompanied the American officer to the other side. This officer told him he should simply take some civilian car; they would give him enough gasoline, and he could try to reach the British Zone. He found a Mercedes in a garage and just took it, over the owner's protest. After even more adventures, he did reach the British Zone, and found his own unit, now billeted in a German base in Hamburg. He reported to his sergeant, who was so surprised he was speechless. He had believed all of them had been killed. Unfortunately, the sergeant had to inform him that his wife had been killed in London in an air raid. That was an especially hard blow of fate for him. He was granted leave, then left the army. In the meantime, he had remarried. This was his story—I suggested to him that he should write a book about it.

Both sets of the Gattungs' parents still lived in Germany, Mrs. Gattung's parents in Ludwigsburg in the corner house just to the south of the garrison church on the top floor. After we had coffee, we wrote letters to our families. Now I could write without being censored. We all reported the unexpected reunion. Night drew nigh; I had to be back in camp by 10:00 PM. When there was only half an hour left, Mr. Gattung assured me that we had plenty of time. I got more and more impatient and told Mr. Gattung he would have to bear the responsibility, because I wasn't going to make it back in time. And then, shortly before 10:00 PM, a taxi arrived and got me back by curfew after all. Another surprise: the cab driver also spoke German and was originally from the Black Forest. Mrs. Gattung told me I was always welcome to visit them any time, if I could manage it. A wonderful day ended for me, but it also made me aware that I was still a POW.

Starting in January 1947, a new regulation was announced, allowing us to leave the camp on Sunday afternoons. The only conditions were: no contact with women, no farther than three miles from camp, no movies or visits to pubs, no public transport, and decent behavior in public. Well, at least it was a little bit of freedom. My first trip was to visit the Gattungs, who were glad to see me. In the meantime, they had learned from their parents that my parents had brought them some food, although they weren't yet able to send packages from England. Everything my parents had done for their parents, they were now eager to pay back in kind.

Their children still kept their distance from me and even avoided me. One Sunday when I was invited to the Gattungs' for dinner, Mrs. Gattung said to me how sorry she was that I always had to wear my POW uniform when I came to visit. Her husband was about my size, and perhaps I might wear something of his, she thought. I agreed right away. Mr. Gattung wasn't home and the children were at Sunday school. I changed clothes in their bedroom, and everything fit, even the shoes. That was quite a feeling, to be wearing civilian clothes again and to look like a normal human being once more. I hardly recognized myself in the mirror. I proudly came downstairs, where Mrs. Gattung was waiting for me. She too was pleasantly surprised by my appearance. I sat by myself in their living room until dinner. Then the children got back from Sunday school. They stopped in their tracks at the door when they saw me. They came over to me, now quite friendly, and shook hands. That broke the ice, and now they treated me like a human being. The fourteen-year-old in particular was completely transformed; now they hardly wanted to leave my side. It actually got a little embarrassing.

That afternoon, we all went to the movies, even though it was prohibited for me. The three of us sat upstairs in the bus in the front seats. When the conductor came forward, I pointed back, as if to say, Daddy's paying for all of us. At the movies, I sat between the two children. You didn't go to the movies in England just for one film; two were shown, one after the other. The first one was harmless, but the second one was a nasty propaganda movie against the Germans, in which German spies landed secretly in England and brutally killed children. The audience really got worked up. I think if they had known that a German was sitting amongst them, they'd have lynched me. Even during the movie, the British got up and left the theater for their "cuppa." At the end of the film, everyone rose and sang the national anthem, so I did, too, of course. I had to be careful not to raise my arm in the Hitler salute.

THREE MEN FROM BERLIN

We had three Berliners in our camp who were inseparable, although they were all different characters. One was a real fatso with a short brush cut. The second was a very young, small, wiry fellow with curly black hair, and the third was a regular beanpole. They were always in good spirits and ready for any prank. The little one's smart Berlin mouth was never still. They worked with a fairly large detail in Hyde Park, cleaning the paths, raking leaves in autumn, shoveling snow and ice in wintertime. These three didn't get much done, however, but just messed around in the park during the workday. They always had plenty of English money. I asked them once how they happened to have so much money all the time. They said they were frequently approached by men in the park looking for encounters with other men. If they paid well, the Berliners would disappear into the bushes with them for a little rendezvous. I couldn't tell whether this was really true, but I suspect they actually went out on robbery escapades at night, since we all knew they were often not in their beds at night.

Our commandant must have heard something about them, and he wanted to check it out. He slipped into their barracks after midnight and found out they weren't there. This time I'll catch them, he thought. His guards had checked the outer fences the day before and had found a hole in the fence hidden by shrubbery. They also found tracks indicating that the hole was being used. This is where they would have to come back in. He hid in the shrubs and kept his eye on the hole and waited patiently, not giving up until dawn. They couldn't possibly come back this late. But just to be sure, he checked their beds once more—and there all three of them were, sound asleep.

He was enraged as he woke them up, and they looked at him groggily. He let them have it: he knew they had been out that night, so how had they gotten back to bed? Innocently, they insisted that was impossible; they'd been in bed all night. The commandant got even more furious. Everyone else in the barracks woke up and was paying close attention to what was going on. He said he'd seen with his own eyes that they hadn't been in bed. Well, then they must have been in the latrine, they said. All that thin tea they drank made them often have to get up in the middle of the night, they responded innocently. But not all three at once, the commandant yelled. Why not? they said, we all drink the same amount of tea. At that point, he just gave up and stormed angrily out of the barracks.

The next morning at roll call, he had the three of them step forward and gave them a stern disciplinary lecture, although only the short one could understand it, since only he spoke English. The commandant promised that they would be the very last men to leave this camp; he would make sure of that. He'd slam the gate behind them. Like little innocent lambs, the three of them stood there with bowed heads, but a little smile could be seen on their faces.

In England, the winter of 1946–1947 was terribly cold. Ponds and rivers froze solid. The three Berliners were again with their detail in Hyde Park, just wandering around, as usual. Suddenly they saw a horse in the under-brush; it had broken through the ice at the lake's edge and was trying wildly to free itself, but sinking deeper and deeper. There was no one around, so they jumped into the water to the thrashing horse and tried to free it, but then broke through themselves. Luckily, the lake at that point wasn't very deep. With enormous effort, they finally managed to get the horse onto dry land, where it stood quite calmly. In the meantime, a lot of passersby had gathered, and a policeman saw what was happening and came over.

There the three of them stood, soaking wet, with their clothes freezing on their bodies, not knowing what to do. The policeman reacted quickly, ran to the nearest telephone, and called an ambulance. A few minutes later, it arrived. The three men were taken away in the warm vehicle, and only then was it learned that they were German POWs. The ambulance raced with blinking light and howling siren through London traffic, back to the camp. They all took a hot bath immediately and put on dry clothes, and that was the end of it. Apart from the sniffles, none of them was harmed by it, and they didn't mention the whole affair again.

Instead of Repatriation, to Labor Camps in England

The following Sunday, right before lunch, a motorcade drove into the camp. Great excitement—what was up now? The three Berliners were called to the office over the PA system. There they were filmed for the weekly newsreel, with speeches made to them. Representatives of the city of London, the government, the RSPCA, the newsreel, and many others had shown up to honor the three men for their heroic deed. They received a certificate and medals, and government officials assured them that they would be released immediately. They would get their walking papers within days. All three were genuinely moved and almost cried; but the commandant's face was emotionless, since he'd promised them the exact opposite. The cars drove away again, and the heroes remained. One has to keep in mind that the British are real fanatics about horses, and a deed like this was, in fact, truly heroic. And two days later, their papers actually were there. They were picked up by a jeep. With a bittersweet smile, the commandant said goodbye to them. He was privately quite proud of having such heroes in his camp and having his camp get so much publicity through the newsreels and the official visit.

Back to our work. One half of a duplex right behind the Grosvenor Hotel near Hyde Park had to be cleared. As usual, I reported to the female officer who gave instructions, and my men started work. The officer conversed with me and said she thought I was awfully young. Older than she was, I insisted, but she wouldn't believe it. After a long conversation, we found out we had the exact same birthday. Here, too, I used my usual pitch: if there was anything left over from dinner, etc., and here there was also plenty to eat. We were even permitted to eat in her living room. Girls kept coming into the room with something or other to do, coincidentally. One would clean the windows (during her lunch break), another would dust the doors, and it was obvious that they were only coming in because of us. My men used their little bits of English, which always sounded amusing.

Then one particularly pretty girl came into the room. All of us looked at her eagerly, some making flirtatious remarks, roughly "she'd fit me just fine," and "she'd be nice company for some pleasant hours." Of course I wouldn't translate what they said, and she just laughed. Later, when I ran into her in the hallway, she spoke to me in perfect German, and I was horrified. She must have understood every single word, I realized, and in embarrassment I made excuses for my men. But she just laughed and said she knew what men were like. I asked her how she happened to speak

German so well, and she told me she had been born a German in Berlin and had gone to school there. She had just managed to flee before her parents were picked up and taken to Auswitsch [*sic,* Auschwitz] where they had been gassed. Here in England, she had joined the army to contribute in her modest way to the destruction of Germany. But when she met such a nice young fellow as me, she said, she couldn't be filled with hatred anymore. She came from a Jewish family. I had to tell my men that, and at first they were shocked, but then they understood everything, and I could calm them down.

As often as she could, she came to visit us. We happened to have two more young men from Berlin in our group, which led to lively conversations and the exchanging of memories. The girl was quite happy to have a chance to use her native language again for a change. The female officer, however, was not only interested in our work; she was also interested in me. To be alone with me, she asked me to repair her electric iron and other things in the office. But all of that was merely a ruse. It finally got to the point where she actually wanted to marry me. But in Gross-Sachsenheim, I already had a girlfriend (later my wife). I promised her, if that didn't work out, I'd come back to her—but it did work out. When she saw my worn-out gloves, she knitted me a new pair of olive drab ones. A female British officer knitting a pair of gloves for a German POW—probably a unique occurrence in the British army. When I shared my reservations with her, that she was used to giving orders, but I was not used to obeying, she insisted that she was quite different in private life. She was pretty and slender, with dark hair she had to hide under a military cap, and her uniform didn't show her figure to its advantage. She painted a shared future for us in the rosiest of colors. Her father owned a farm but was old and frail, and he desperately needed help, she said. In response to my objection that I didn't know anything about farming, she said I wouldn't have to work, because they had enough staff; I would just have to manage things. I later learned that not everything she told me was quite true, but we still write to each other at Christmas.

A SAD EVENT

When it was freezing cold in February, I came down with a bad cold and a high fever, and had to go into the infirmary. An elderly man from Saxony was our medic, rather chubby, with a military haircut, a very amiable fellow who always took good care of his patients and always had a joke ready, which he told in Saxon dialect. He was a very good medic (I suspect he had been a doctor) and only called for a civilian doctor in the most severe cases. There were eight of us in the infirmary, and it was toasty warm; our medic really spoiled us. On my last day, he didn't make his rounds. We waited a while, but still he didn't come, and we gradually got worried and asked in the office where he was, but no one had seen him. We went looking for him. Then came a cry from the furnace room. We ran over there, and one of the POWs was standing there with his knees shaking, pointing at a man. Our medic was hanging over the water heater from a pipe, with staring eyes and his tongue sticking out, the tips of his shoes just touching the floor, dead. We couldn't grasp it. We cut him down and took him into the infirmary. The news went around the camp like wildfire. No one could understand it, not even his best friends—why had he done it?

THE SAFE

In one estate, there was only the safe to be taken away. Safes are notoriously very heavy and hard to handle with their rounded corners. We took beams and ropes with us, since it was upstairs. Elegant homes of the English upper class were all built similarly. One entered through a gate with columns into a great hall with a very high ceiling, elegantly furnished, various colors of marble flooring, giant mirrors at head height, reaching almost to the ceiling, and lots of wall fixtures with three to four electric lights each. The owners had taken their curtains and paintings with them. A wide marble staircase led to the second floor where the private rooms of the owners were, the railings of artistic wrought iron. From the second floor, a narrow staircase went up to the third story, where the servants lived. The kitchen was in the cellar. When all the lights were on in the salon, reflecting in all the mirrors, it was a fantastic sight. You could easily imagine the kind of magnificent parties that had been held here.

Now, however, the rooms were empty, except for the safe we were supposed to pick up, which belonged to the army. On beams, we pushed it as far as the stairs and fastened ropes to it. We cautiously maneuvered it onto another beam, which we'd placed on the marble staircase to protect it. Somehow or other, it slipped off sideways, and the men let go of the rope. The safe bumped down, gathering speed, down the stairs, chipping the edge off every step, and landed downstairs on the marble floor, smashing a large piece of it. It looked terrible. The men just stood there with awkward smiles; they'd slipped and hadn't been able to hold it. I understood; they, too, might not get their release papers now. I wasn't willing to take responsibility for this, though. After a short discussion with our driver, I had him take me to our boss at the War Ministry, where I reported the accident. He had to see it for himself and drove with us to the house to look at the damage. The men gave a sober report, deadly serious and very rueful, of how it had happened. With their rubber soles, they had slipped on the smooth floor and had not been able to hold on to the safe with all their might. They were terribly sorry, they said, and they begged his pardon. Our boss was almost in tears from all our apologizing, but I knew better. Well, there's nothing to be done about it now, he said. The main thing is, nothing happened to any of you. And then he drove back to his office. Finishing the loading went smoothly. We didn't need to worry about the driver, who knew exactly how it had happened.

All of our drivers were ardent communists and couldn't stand the rich. They complained about everything, the government and the officials they had to prop up with their meager wages. I once said I thought the monarchy and King George the Sixth were superfluous and just cost the taxpayers a lot of money. But then, suddenly, they got quite serious. Leave the monarchy out of it, they said; we need them and want to keep them. I was quite surprised.

DANCING

The next day, another house had to be emptied, in Belgravia, near Victoria Station. About twenty girls were still there and were assigned to help us; that would be fun. In the salon stood a snow-white piano, which must have belonged to the house's owner. The girls asked me to play something. But I didn't know how to play the piano, apart from a single song as a duet, "The Boy Saw the Little Rose" ["Sah ein Knab ein Röslein stehn"]. I played that with feeling, all three verses, and was at the end of my repertoire. Everyone clapped and demanded more, but I didn't know anything else.

And then our driver happened to sit down at the piano. What a surprise; he could really play and started pounding the keys until the house rocked. Soon I sensed that my men were eager to do a little dancing, since they'd all stopped work. As if by command, each of them picked out a girl, and the dancing started. That worked beautifully on the smooth marble floor, and the girls participated enthusiastically. They were all about our age or younger; we weren't enemies anymore, and there were no class differences; we just danced close together.

Our driver played on tirelessly: waltzes, tangos, marches, etc. The dancing got wilder and wilder, and we changed partners, so that all the girls got a chance. Even those who didn't really know how to dance very well got pulled onto the dance floor, and we sang all the current English pop tunes. For the first time in a long while, the men held girls in their arms again, and they made the most of it; the girls certainly didn't seem to mind at all.

But I was starting to get a little nervous, in case an officer or our boss should show up; then things might get unpleasant for us and for the girls. So I went outside and stood watch at the front door. You could still hear the music, the singing, and the girls' laughter outside. Passersby stopped and asked me what was going on in there; I said I didn't have any idea.

After an hour of this, I had to put an end to it; we still had a long trip back to the depot ahead of us and had to be there in time for our return trip home. Everybody was sweating; the driver was exhausted, but happy that everyone had had such a good time. Even if the girls in their uniforms and with their hair up under their caps didn't look particularly sexy, they were still flesh-and-blood girls. Since the work at this house was finished, we didn't see these girls again, unfortunately. I'm sure they recall this little dancing episode fondly.

For one of our jobs, we went to Wellington Barracks, near Buckingham Palace. The royal guard is stationed in these barracks and performs the famous Changing of the Guard at 11:00 AM every day, which attracts many tourists. In the barracks yard, a British officer approached me directly and asked whether I was a German, to which I responded that I was. He wanted to know where I'd served, and I told him, in Tunisia, against the British. He became more curious and wanted to know exactly where. I told him it had been near Beja. He said he'd been there, too. It turned out that he and his men had been directly opposite us. I had shot at his men during their retreat, but I didn't tell him that.

He got quite excited, and I had to go with him to the officers' club, where he introduced me to his fellow officers. We spent a long time recounting how things had been, and it was interesting to hear his version of the battle. I also realized how poorly equipped we had been. Meanwhile, my people were done with their job and were looking everywhere for me. They needed to load some sacks of coal into a warehouse.

THE ROLLS ROYCE

In London, we ran into a detail from another camp, and I happened to ask whether a certain Franz Ertl was among them. They said, yes, there was a Franz Ertl in their camp; it was my friend, and their camp was only three miles away from ours. We would be able to meet up again. I told them to let him know I'd meet him on Sunday afternoon at 2:00 PM at the church in the village between the two camps. We were delighted to see each other once more; we met many times after that and took some long hikes.

One Sunday, he came to pick me up at my camp, and I was waiting at the appointed time at the front gate. I was looking for him on the road when a black Rolls Royce open touring car pulled up and stopped on the other side of the road. I heard my name called, "Walter," and went over—it was Franz who was riding in a Rolls Royce.

What a surprise that was! He told me to get in, but I could hardly believe my eyes. After we said hello, he introduced me to the driver, whom I then greeted in the British style, without shaking hands, which wasn't customary there. An elderly gentleman with gray, almost white hair, a handlebar mustache, a white snap-brim cap on his head, wearing driving goggles, sat at the wheel. Franz and I sat in the back in seats so lavishly upholstered we almost sank in them. The car drove off, almost like a silent cloud, the engine barely audible. I felt like a king as we headed out into the country. I wanted to know from Franz what this was all about, mainly whether this gentleman was a foreigner. It was rather odd to have a gentleman like that chauffeuring two young German POWs around in a Rolls Royce. Franz told me to calm down and related the story. While he'd been working in London, this old fellow had spoken to him and had invited him to lunch. He lived in a little castle not far from the camp, with an estate attached to it. In the war, he'd been a general, but now he lived alone in his castle, without any family. A cook and a butler took care of him.

Apparently he was fascinated with Franz, who was a good-looking fellow. He loved Franz's casual style and could speak a little bit of German, which he liked to use. He kept inviting him to lunch, followed usually by a drive out into the countryside. He'd also given him quite a few presents. Franz was simply a welcome change of routine for the old man in his lonely life. Even though Franz still couldn't speak much English, the two of them got along fine.

We stopped at a roadside pub and went in, naturally as the driver's guests. Toward evening, they brought me back to the camp, right to the gate. The POWs and the sentries at the gate were amazed when they saw me get out, which I enjoyed, of course. I met Franz many more times, although he had less and less time; in the meantime, he also had an English girlfriend. He had still never received any news from his parents.

THEFT

Every day, a group drove along with us from the camp into the city, to work in Victoria Station. Their job was to unload the packages that English soldiers had sent from Germany to their families and to open them under supervision. The contents were checked, and then the packages were resealed by our people. There were often valuables in them, such as watches, rings, and costly jewelry, which surely had not always been acquired legitimately in Germany. Without any pangs of conscience, the POWs took this and that surreptitiously. That went along fine until one British officer came to pick up the package he had recently sent from Germany himself.

He opened it on the spot and realized that a valuable watch was missing. It must have been stolen by one of the POWs. He gave the alarm, and all the POWs were locked in a small room. MPs were called, who searched everyone thoroughly, without finding anything. The MPs then wanted to go to the camp and search there. Meanwhile, the truck had arrived to take these men and us back to camp. These men would be taken to camp by the police, he was told.

Our driver put it quickly in gear and raced to us. We leapt aboard, and the last man had hardly made it when he stepped on the gas, but he didn't drive the usual route because of the heavy traffic. Since he was a Londoner, he knew alternate routes. He wanted to make it to camp before the police did. Driving at a breakneck speed, ignoring red lights, going the wrong way on one-way streets, we actually did reach camp before the police. We got out quickly and ran into the barracks and alarmed everyone, searching through all the bedding and personal belongings of the other POWs. A lot of stolen goods turned up and were quickly buried in the yard. When the police got there, everything was gone, and they found nothing. They left again, disappointed. The other POWs were grateful for our quick reaction.

Later, it turned out that the driver was himself involved, which was why he had been in such a hurry.

American headquarters in London, just off Oxford Street, urgently needed a few bags of coal for the kitchen stoves. We delivered them. It was a huge building complex in the old Victorian style with a covered portico over the entrance. We drove up to the front door and found two sentries with machine guns, who sent me down to the kitchen, where I reported to the chef. He told me in English where to dump the coal. Then he asked me whether we were Germans. When I said yes, he spoke Viennese dialect to me. He was a Viennese in the U.S. Army. Naturally I asked immediately whether he had anything left over for us to eat. Of course, he said, as much as you want; just go into that empty room, and he'd bring it. Shortly thereafter, he showed up with a huge tray full of the finest things: roasts, noodles, salads, everything to inspire a German's taste buds, and plenty of beer and Coke. He sat down with us, pleased that we liked the food, and told us his story. As a Jew, he had left Austria after Hitler had come to power and immigrated to America. As a chef, he had managed to get through the war quite well. Finally, when we couldn't eat or drink another thing, he told us we could come by any time we liked, and there would always be something for us to eat. But my men should always go to the back room; only I should report to him. No one was supposed to see the others. Again, we had a good feeding station, and we made plenty of use of it.

Another time, I was standing bored on the sidewalk. An elegant elderly lady with a cane walked up to me and asked in a sullen tone whether I was a German. I said, "Yes, madam," and she went away without another word. A few minutes later, she returned, looked at me haughtily, walked up to me, and handed me a small package. Without stopping, she walked on. I was so surprised that all I could call out after her was "thank you." In the package were cigarettes and cigars.

Automobile traffic was very heavy in the inner city, especially in the evening. The truck that usually took us back to camp stopped across the road. So the twelve of us had to cross busy Whitehall Street. This was not easy with the endless stream of traffic. I walked up to the nearest policeman in Trafalgar Square and asked him to help us cross the street, which he gladly did. Eventually, there was always someone there to help us.

Scotland Yard, near Whitehall, also urgently needed some sacks of coal delivered. It was quite a special occasion to enter this famous building. It took me a while to find the porter. Nothing to eat there, and no tip, either. But in front of the main entrance to Victoria Station, at the stationmaster's office, we could always get a cup of tea and a piece of cake.

We were in the city every day, and I learned my way around quite well, almost all the streets, squares, and buildings, although I didn't know what was in all of them. I asked our boss whether he, as a city council-lor, would be willing to show us the city and explain what everything was. He said he'd be glad to. But then for weeks nothing happened. Finally I told him we had learned in school that English gentlemen always keep their promises. That was quite right, he said, and asked why I had brought it up. I said someone had once promised to show me London, but appar-ently that someone hadn't been a gentleman. Now he got it and laughed out loud. I meant him, he realized. He said we'd do it the next day, if the weather were decent.

The weather was fine the next day, and we could start our sightseeing tour. The boss sat next to the driver, and we sat in the back of the truck. Through the open sliding roof, he explained all the sights to me, and I trans-lated into German for my comrades. We spent the entire day driving around the city, even to the slums in South London. He told us to take off our German caps before we went there, though, since the slum residents were more strongly anti-German. It was their part of London that had taken more German bombs, whereas the West End had been relatively spared. That was true; very few bombs fell near Whitehall and Westminster. Buckingham Palace was only slightly damaged in one corner, and only a side tower of Parliament was hit. St. Paul's Cathedral had also survived almost undamaged, although the entire surrounding area was reduced to ashes by one air raid.

I had seen this conflagration back in Germany before I had left, in a newsreel, with everything on fire at night, and in the middle, lit by the flames, stood the dome of St. Paul's. My boss told me that, when everything around the cathedral was on fire, the Thames, from which water was pumped for firefighting, was at its lowest level in human memory that night, and the pump intakes didn't reach all the way to the water, so the fire department had had no way of putting out the fire.

On our tour, we were shown all the sights of the city, but we weren't allowed to enter any of the buildings, including the Tower of London. I was not able to make up for that until forty-five years later. We thanked our boss and driver sincerely and ended a fine day.

One rainy evening, I was waiting on the sidewalk for our ride home, with the lights of the cars reflected in wet Whitehall Street and pedestrians hurrying to and fro. An elderly man in worn clothing walked past me slowly, then stopped, and came back. He took me by the sleeve and pulled me into a doorway. I was trying to pull free, when he asked me quite calmly if I were a German. "Yes," I said, "why?" He said he was an Irishman, and he still admired Hitler; he took a £10 note out of his pocket and pressed it into my hand and walked away. All I could do was say "thank you."

In May 1947, it was finally spring again, and we could enjoy the sun after a long winter. Well-dressed and cheerful people were strolling in the parks, and the first sunbathers were lying on the grass in Hyde Park. I'd been behind barbed wire for four whole years. A few rumors kept circulating that the English were thinking of letting us go soon. From home, we heard that things were desperate, but that people were glad to be rid of National Socialism. The largest part of the damage had been cleared away, but there was no thought yet of reconstruction. There were shortages of everything, but people were starting to hope again.

We had to observe everything in Germany from a distance. Our living conditions were bearable in England, but we finally wanted to be free again. We now could leave the camp in the evening, but what was there to do? We weren't permitted to go to the movies, and it was too far to downtown London. But I could visit the Gattung family. Mr. Gattung gladly lent me his bicycle, and I took a number of trips into the countryside, although I had to pay close attention to riding on the left-hand side of the road. Most POWs stayed in camp and played cards or chess with friends. There were no planned activities as there had been in the American camp, no language classes, no lectures, only a nondenominational religious service on Sunday morning in the small camp chapel, conducted by a pastor from another camp.

Now there were no more coal transport jobs, but there were still houses to be emptied. We all had enough English money, despite the prohibition, but we couldn't buy much. Even after two years of peace, most grocery items in England were still rationed. We had some additional food almost every day in the city either with the girls or the Americans, so we weren't hungry. I frequently visited the Gattungs and sometimes took along a friend.

ILLEGAL BUSINESS

Of the three drivers who took us around to jobs, the youngest was my age. He was assigned to this duty and was always trying to make some kind of deal. We were involved in a lot of deals with him, dividing up the profits half for him, half for us. We soon realized that there were no checks of what and how much we had delivered in the depot where we dropped things off. Now we were having to empty out and dismantle entire barracks. In many of London's parks during the war, anti-aircraft bunkers had been built to defend against German air raids. Now they were not needed. The AA artillery had long been removed, but the barracks and their inventory were still there.

Our driver had good connections everywhere. When we took out bathtubs, showers, washbasins, or electrical wiring and fixtures, most of it was sold to junk dealers. From the empty houses we regularly pulled out the lead piping that connected the wall-mounted flush tanks to the toilets. Lead was highly sought by dealers. One time we had a load of lead pipe to sell to a scrap dealer. He sent us in back to unload, where we discovered a lot of copper cable. While one group unloaded the lead pipe, another group loaded the copper cable into the truck, since we knew the dealers usually didn't pay any attention to trucks as they left. The driver got the money at the gate, and we drove to the next dealer with our new load.

Our driver was quite a practical joker. On one rather busy corner, we had to empty a house, and while the men were working, we just stood around on the sidewalk. He discovered the switch box that controlled the traffic lights. We stood in front of it as he took out a special wrench, opened the box, and turned something. All of the lights immediately turned red, and all traffic came to a stop. On all four streets, the lines got longer and longer, and drivers started honking their horns, but no one dared to drive off against the light. Then we just walked away and watched the traffic jam from a distance, until finally the police noticed what was wrong and fixed the lights.

At work, we kept noticing the olive-drab quilts on the girls' beds; we'd had quilts just like this in America. Out of curiosity, I looked at one of them closely and found a German name written on it in indelible ink. As I had suspected, they were our quilts that the English had so greedily taken away from us, and now they'd ended up here—poor England. A girl had been watching me and wanted to know whose name that was; she, too, had wondered about it. I examined every quilt I saw, hoping to find my own again.

Before we had left America, everyone had labeled his quilt with indelible ink. They hadn't even been cleaned. The girls were happy to have one at all, since they were certainly better than their scratchy wool blankets.

THE BARRACKS

In late May, we heard that England was planning to release its POWs in the order in which they had been taken prisoner. That seemed right, and I figured my chances were pretty good, since I had been taken prisoner in North Africa in 1943. So it could only be a matter of weeks now.

First, however, we had to dismantle three barracks in South London in a little park. This had been an AA battery with housing for the crew. Initially, we took everything out, tubs, showers, radiators, etc. We sold it all on the black market. Then the barracks themselves were to be broken up and taken to the depot.

The driver had already found a taker for one of the barracks. While we took two of them apart, we left the best one intact so that it could be erected again. This one we intended to take away on a flatbed truck one Sunday and sell. That was potentially dangerous. Since my release date was already fixed, I didn't want to participate in this risky undertaking myself and endanger my release. But I did discuss the plan with the driver. On the last workday before Sunday, the men would leave their overalls in the truck with the driver. On Sunday morning, they'd go separately as pedestrians to a different place and be met by our driver. They'd get in, put on their overalls, load the parts of the barracks onto the flatbed truck, and off they'd go. After it had been delivered, the driver would bring them back, they'd take off their overalls, and walk back to camp.

Everything had been worked out. The loading went fine, and off they drove, but when they came to a railroad underpass, the gable ends were too tall and got stuck. They fell off the truck onto the road. The whole road was blocked and traffic started backing up. There was nothing to be done but to drag the individual pieces by hand through the underpass and reload them on the other side. Soon the police became aware of the traffic jam. They offered their help, and several drivers also lent a hand, and soon everything was reloaded. The men were sweating blood in case the police wanted to know details. The driver walked some distance away and waited, but then the rest of the trip was uneventful. Later, he told me that people had been upset to see POWs having to work on a Sunday two years after the war.

Everything worked out, and everyone made quite a bit of money. The following Monday morning, when this barracks building was supposed to be transported away, I feigned surprise to discover that it had been stolen. That was an outrage, and I would have to tell my boss about it right away. We drove to him and reported the incredible theft. He had to see for himself and came back with us. When he saw that it was gone, he complained about his countrymen, and we did too, about how English morality had sunk so low. He wanted to know all the details; he and I went to all the neighboring houses and asked whether they'd seen anything. Everyone agreed that they'd seen soldiers in overalls taking away the pieces of the barracks and had wondered why they were working on Sunday (we wore the same overalls as the British soldiers). It apparently didn't dawn on him that it might have been us, or maybe he didn't want to know. When he was gone, we had a good laugh.

CAMP ENFIELD

Our camp in the middle of Enfield was surrounded by homes where there were a lot of girls, so friendships with POWs were not unlikely. None of us left camp without looking our best, with combed hair, ironed uniforms, polished shoes, and on our best behavior; the girls liked that.

Our shirts had no collars, so we cut a piece out of the back of the shirt and made it into a collar. There was a small sewing machine in the camp, and we used this for the tedious sewing tasks. I even made a necktie out of some blue curtain material. However, we couldn't take our jackets off. Since physical contact with women was forbidden, there were always amusing scenes at the camp gate when Germans came back with girlfriends. For their goodnight kiss, the men stood stiffly, and the girls kissed them and gave them a hug. This way the guards couldn't intervene, since English girls couldn't be forbidden to kiss Germans.

THE MISSED WEDDING

I had never seen any of the royal family, but now an opportunity presented itself. Across from the front portal of Westminster Abbey we were assigned to empty the office of the YMCA, with our truck right in front of the building. Noon approached, and more and more people were gathering in front of the church. Our driver went to ask why. At 12:00 noon there was going to be a wedding in Westminster Abbey. Winston Churchill's daughter was getting married, and members of the royal family were going to attend.

We had the perfect location and could see everything from the back of our truck. A huge crowd assembled, it was almost noon, and they would be here any minute. At that moment, a policeman came up to us and ordered us to leave the square instantly; we were a security risk. Our pleas were to no avail, and we had to leave. But generally, the British people were not afraid of us; they were used to having POWs in their country, and as long as we didn't draw attention to ourselves, they ignored us.

RELEASE

Finally, my name was on the release list for 28 May 1947. I could hardly wait for the day to come; at long last, my dream of freedom was about to become reality. With my English money I bought everything imaginable outside: cans of coffee, cocoa, tea, chocolate, soap, sweetener, shoelaces, sewing gear, etc. I had already had most of these things from America. I took leave of my boss, and the parting was hard for both of us; we had gotten to be good friends, and I promised to write to him soon.

Sadly and gladly at once, I said goodbye to the Gattung family. Eric was sorry that he wouldn't have anyone left to help with dirty jobs. Mr. Gattung promised that they would visit their parents in Germany as soon as it was possible, and then they would see me, too. I was also able to say goodbye to that officer who had wanted to marry me. I promised her that I would come back if things didn't work out with my girlfriend. Of my friend Franz in the other camp, all I knew was that he was also going to be released soon. The long-awaited day drew ever nearer. On the one hand, London had become a kind of second home to me, but on the other hand, I was really looking forward to being free at last. The days passed too slowly.

LEAVING ENFIELD

And then the day arrived. I was picked up with twenty other POWs in a truck. It was an exhilarating feeling to say goodbye to the others and the camp leader and leave the camp. We drove through the now familiar streets of London and went to a release camp in the southwest, where individual ship transport was being arranged. Another week was spent there, with a growing number of POWs arriving every day. Unexpectedly, I ran into my friend Franz again; he was also about to be released. He still had not heard anything from his parents, but a brother had written him that he should come to Bavaria. In this camp, too, we were able to go out, on the usual conditions. We took two long hikes, just to get away from the crowd.

OTTO RÖSSLEN

One mild evening, while I was taking a walk around camp, I heard a voice behind me calling "Walter." I turned around but couldn't see anyone I knew, so I kept going; he must have meant someone else. Then, a second time, "Walter, don't you know me?" Again, I looked back, and there was Otto Rösslen, from my hometown. We greeted each other warmly; it was the first of my acquaintances from home whom I had seen during my whole military service and imprisonment. Otto Rösslen was an old friend, born in 1906, who had a farm in Gross-Sachsenheim and a cartage business with his brown horse. He always brought our coal and wood from the forest, and plowed our land. He was always a tireless worker. He was popular with young and old people alike, always friendly. He and his horse were part of our town. He wasn't in this camp to be released, but had to work here. As a stoker, he had to provide heat and hot water. Every evening, we sat together. He had lots to tell me about home, since he'd been drafted quite late in the war. This brought back a lot of memories.

SWIMMING

This period was quite hot, with the sun shining in a cloudless sky, as we impatiently waited to start our trip home, and the days were long. Franz and I took another long hike and were quite a ways from camp when we came upon a fairly wide river, full to its banks. We decided to have a swim, and since there was no one around, we just went in naked. We made a pile of our clothes and dove in. It was wonderfully refreshing, and we played around like kids, with races and diving. We forgot the time until we gradually realized that the banks seemed rather high above us; that seemed strange, but we didn't think anything more of it. But then we felt a peculiar tugging, and the water flowed faster and faster. Now we had to get out, but it wasn't easy. The banks were now some fifteen feet high and slick with mud. We had difficulty crawling out. But we didn't know where we were; the region was completely foreign to us, and not a trace of our clothes. There we stood, smeared from head to toe with mud, no water to wash off with; we couldn't very well go back in the river.

111

Then it dawned on us that the river flowed into the nearby sea, and the tides were making the river level change. We'd gotten in at high tide; but the water was ebbing back out to sea and it would soon be low tide again, so our clothes would have to be lying where we'd left them. We ran along until we saw a something white in the distance; it was our clothes. But we couldn't get dressed while we were all muddy. So we took bunches of grass and rubbed the worst of it off each other; luckily there was no one around. We got dressed carefully and hurried back to camp without meeting anyone. Once we were finally under the shower, we could breathe easy.

After a week of impatient waiting in this camp, we moved out. Otto Rösslen gave me coffee, tea, and ten pencils for his sister Marie; I was glad to take it, but it was subtracted from my allowable ration. Again, our luggage was checked; one full sea bag was allowed per person. We started in the early morning. A passenger train was waiting for us at the nearby station. The train took us up north to the port city of Hull on the east coast. For the last time, we traveled through England, everyone in good spirits; this time, we weren't going to be deceived. It was June and already quite warm, and the scent of new-mown hay came through the open windows, with the meadows being mown everywhere.

It was evening by the time we reached Hull. The train rolled into the port, where a troop transport ship was waiting for us. It was very crowded, but we didn't care now, if only we were headed for Germany. We could hardly stand the anticipation; everyone was already home in his thoughts. What would we find there? How would everything look? Everyone was so excited they couldn't sleep; we all stayed up on deck. A light breeze was blowing on this starry night.

We kept hearing bell buoys in the far distance, marking sunken ships; most of them hadn't been raised yet. When it got light, we all looked for land. Where would we be arriving? The ship docked at the Alte Liebe pier in Cuxhaven, and we got our first depressing view. In the inner harbor lay half-sunken ships, ruins everywhere. No one was there to welcome us, and our good mood evaporated. We disembarked across a temporary gangplank and were finally on German soil again, in our Germany. Our sea bags had been loaded onto the train and transferred to the ship, but we didn't see them now. We hoped they would be shipped to us, or had we been tricked again?

Instead of Repatriation, to Labor Camps in England

A passenger train was waiting for us at the harbor. We quickly got aboard. British soldiers were still giving us orders; we were still POWs. The train had no seating. We departed and arrived in Hamburg an hour later, with a brief layover in the totally destroyed central train station. Everything looked terrible; the huge glass roof had been destroyed, ruins wherever we looked, burned-out buildings, nothing but ruins. And yet, everywhere there was life. People were walking around through the ruins without paying them any heed. But no one was paying any attention to us, either. The trip continued to the Münster Camp in the Lüneburg Heath. Münster Camp had been a huge establishment for the German army, with a drill field; many soldiers knew it, and even today in the late 1990s, the unified German army is stationed there.

Again, we were assigned to barracks—still not free. Again, we had the old-style German toilets, meals from the field kitchen, one-pot dishes. The German camp administration was running under military-style rules. We weren't used to this anymore, but it wouldn't last long. The next day, our sea bags arrived, and everything was still there. This camp also received POWs from Russia. How desperate they looked, nothing but skin and bones, with swollen heads, dressed in rags, with unshaven stubble. We, on the other hand, were in good shape, had decent clothing, and lots of desirable goods in our sea bags. Not only their external appearance was different, but also their inner being. What had been done to these men?

At first, we wondered why they kept standing around us during our meals outdoors, until we figured out that they were waiting to see if we would have any food left over. We didn't care much for this dull army food anyway, so we were glad to share it with these fellows. One of them was insatiable, very thin, but with a large swollen head; he looked like an old man, but his body didn't seem to fit him. We asked how old he was: sixteen. We wished we could have really fed him well, but his friends warned us that it might kill him; his body wouldn't be able to take it.

There was also a movie theater in the camp that showed old sentimental German movies. We sat on the benches, but those who were returning from Russia wouldn't sit next to us. They squatted in the aisles and sat on the floor. Nothing we said would help; they just stared at us with their hollow cheeks and uncomprehending eyes. This was painful for us. None of us had chosen the POW camp he'd ended up in; we were all German soldiers. But they seemed to feel like second-class citizens compared to us.

Here I once again met up with my friend Ertl, and we could stay together. We were glad to get moving again; the fate of the returnees from Russia depressed us a lot. Another train without any benches, our first stop in Bebra. A train full of returnees from Russia stopped next to ours. They were stuffed into freight cars. All of them tried to get to the open door to beg us for cigarettes. We had plenty with us, but we wanted to take them home. We gave them some anyway, but we were relieved when the train moved on again.

Just after Bebra, our train stopped on the open line, and we could hardly believe our eyes. A crowd of people, mainly youngsters, came up to our train and decorated it with greenery and colorful paper flags, and wrote on the cars with chalk, "Welcome Home, Returnees," as they waved to us. We almost cried; we hadn't been forgotten after all. We hadn't expected this kind of gesture—it was a real celebration for us. We kept moving, but we saw other things, too. German girls were walking arm in arm with British soldiers and kissing them openly. We yelled at them and called the British soldiers names, but they just grinned, and the girls, just to tease us, hugged the soldiers closer.

Slowly, the train headed south over makeshift wooden trestles, where everything shook, then again through destroyed cities; we didn't know our final destination. That night, no one slept; we were all too excited. The night was warm, and we all leaned out the windows. In Würzburg, we had a longer stop. The train station was totally destroyed; only some of the columns that had supported the roof were still standing. Toward evening, we arrived in Dachau, and the train went to the gate of the notorious concentration camp. Again we were assigned to barracks.

We had stayed in a lot of barracks, but none as grim as these. Narrow, three-tiered wooden bunks, narrow aisles, toilets outside. One water faucet for the entire barracks. A barbed-wire fence stood around each barracks. How had human beings been able to stand this for years? Although we didn't have any lice, everyone got foul-smelling delousing powder sprayed into his clothes. We were still locked up. We could write a card home, though, that we would be there in a few days. Some of us had still not heard from their families; where would they be released? My companion Franz Ertl had his brother's address, at least. Otherwise, I would have taken him home with me.

After four days of waiting, we lined up for our discharge papers. Finally, we had them in our hands, those long-awaited documents, and a free ticket for the train. Each of us had to see a doctor to determine whether he had any war wounds, which had to be reported. Since my wound had healed up fine, I didn't report it, but that turned out to be a mistake. As the years have passed, I have had some pain, and my circulation has gotten worse. I've already had one operation. Since I didn't report it at the time, it hasn't been recognized as a war wound.

Although we had our discharge papers in hand, we still weren't allowed to leave, but had to spend another night in camp. We looked over the train schedules posted on the walls. I found an express train from Munich via Ulm to the Rhineland, with a stop in Bietigheim, leaving Munich at 3:00 PM The next morning, we all pushed toward the gate as it was finally opened and we stepped into freedom. It was an indescribable feeling, being free. The sun shone on us like a smiling greeting from heaven. Reality caught up with us soon, though, since the Dachau station was more than a mile away, and we had our sea bags on our backs. But the people of Dachau were there to help us. They were waiting for us with handcarts, wheelbarrows, children's wagons, and bicycles to help carry our things. Children and elderly people were hoping for a little something such as cigarettes or soap; they'd accept anything in payment. An elderly woman loaded Franz and me and our sea bags onto her handcart. We wanted to help her pull it, but she rejected our offer, apparently fearing a smaller tip.

We took a local train into Munich, but we had several hours' wait until our trains departed. We camped out with many others in the makeshift station, anxiously guarding our luggage so that it wouldn't get stolen. They'd warned us about this in the camp. Since there were two of us, it was easier for one of us to walk around or go to the toilet or stretch his legs. Everyone kept looking at the station clock. Time seemed to drag, and it was quite hot, and we were thirsty. There was nothing to drink for sale, so we had to drink the tap water in the bathroom. Franz returned from a walk, and I set out to see where my train would be leaving from in three hours.

At the platform stood a train, crammed full, no more room in it. I kept walking, and then I saw the sign on one car, "München-Dortmund." This was my train. I quickly ran back, went to the toilet again, and said good-bye to my friend Franz. We'd been together off and on for almost four years. We'd been through a lot together, good times and bad, and we knew we could rely on each other. Now we had to part, but we promised to see each other again soon. A brief handshake, and each of us went his own way.

TRAIN TRIP

There stood my train in the glaring midday heat, with the platform roofs destroyed, and three more hours until departure. I took my sea bag onto the platform and found all the cars full to bursting, but there was no option—I had to find room. I walked along the cars looking for a space to squeeze into. The entranceways were packed, and no one wanted to let anyone else in.

I forced a door open and shoved my sea bag in. They made enough space for me to squeeze in. Maybe they'd be more considerate of me as a just-released POW. I stood right at the door. It was frightfully hot in the car and the air was stale, even though all the windows were open. Still three hours until departure; this would be some treat. I could only get one foot on the floor as I hung out of the window with my upper body, anxiously guarding my sea bag. Most of the passengers had come with knapsacks, suitcases, and handbags from the Ruhr area to Bavaria to go "hamstering," looking for food and things to barter. Hunger had forced them to make the trip. Now they were headed back home; this train was the only connection to their homes. Their luggage also took up space, although some of them simply carried it on their heads, even though they had a longer trip ahead of them than I did. More and more people wanted to get in, but I wouldn't open the door. Time just didn't seem to pass. I was starting to get a cramp standing in the same position, but at least I had some fresh air from the open window, although the sun was shining directly on my head.

Finally at 5:00 PM sharp, the train started rolling slowly; now it could only be a matter of hours until I was home. They would all be in bed by then, since I wouldn't get to Gross-Sachsenheim before midnight. What kind of a reception would I get? What would be waiting for me? My thoughts were agitated as the wheels clicked monotonously; my legs had long since gone to sleep, and I couldn't feel them anymore.

The landscape through which we traveled was unchanged. Farmers were doing their work, and everything looked so peaceful. Five years previously, I had traveled this same route in the opposite direction, hoping to return as a radiant victor after we had won the war. Now I was coming home as a discharged POW.

We went through Augsburg, which didn't look peaceful at all with all its ruins, then on to Ulm, where the cathedral was still standing, but everything else was in ruins. From the station you could see the cathedral clearly through the ruined city. The sun sank slowly on the horizon, and the evening's coolness brought some relief. The passengers in the train slept standing up, since all of them were exhausted. Our next stop was Stuttgart, and by now it was night. Not many people got out, but more wanted to get in. Darkness covered the damaged city. We changed locomotives and continued on.

I had been in the first car, but now I was in the last one. I hoped the train would stop in Bietigheim. Yes, it was braking and stopping. But the platform was on the other side of the train. I couldn't get through and had to climb out on the wrong side. Not climb out, exactly; I had no feeling in my legs and feet. When I finally got the door open, I just fell out with my sea bag. There I lay unable to move. The train rolled away, and the sparse lighting in the station was turned off. There I lay next to the track, waiting until feeling returned to my legs. This wasn't the way I had imagined my homecoming.

Slowly, I was able to get back up and pick up my luggage, feeling my way to the platform in the dark. All of a sudden, a station official was standing in front of me, asking, "Where did you come from? What are you doing here in the middle of the night?" I explained everything to him, and he responded, "It's after midnight. You won't get home before morning." He sensed that I was totally worn out, as he said, "Come into my office; you can sleep on my cot. I'll wake you for the first train in the morning." I was so thankful to this man; I fell asleep immediately, but then he woke me up right away. "Come quickly, there's a locomotive headed toward Mühlacker. I talked to them, and they'll take you along." Sadly, I didn't know who this friendly man was; I'd like to be able to thank him sincerely.

I rode in a locomotive for the first time as it moved very slowly over a wooden trestle. In the moonlight, I saw the outdoor pool at Ellental where I had swum so often, now also completely destroyed. The locomotive rattled over switches, and then we entered Gross-Sachsenheim station. I was at my final destination.

The locomotive had stopped, although the track signal was green, and the stationmaster stormed out of his cabin to the platform and yelled, "Are you blind? Can't you see that it's green?" "Calm down—we've just brought you a returnee from Gross-Sachsenheim," he called back. I quickly gave the two men in the locomotive a few cigarettes and they steamed off.

"Well now, Walter—is it really you?" I heard the stationmaster say. It was my old acquaintance, Kurt Wieland. He gave me a hearty welcome, and I was pleased by the reception. "Hurry on home! Your folks have been waiting for you. You can pick up your sea bag tomorrow morning." I ran quickly through the dark but familiar streets toward Churchyard Lane, with my heart beating in my throat. The starry sky reminded me of the song we often played in America, "The Stars of Home." And then I was standing in front of my home.

Walter Schmid posed for this military portrait in his German uniform early in the war prior to his capture. Courtesy of Walter Schmid.

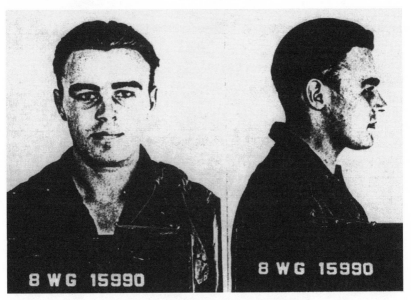

8 WG 15990   8 WG 15990

Picture of Schmid taken by the U.S. Army during his POW processing. His PW number is shown in the frame. Images and their accompanying descriptions were used by the army to identify prisoners and circulated among troops and the media if they escaped. From Walter Schmid's POW record in the Deutsche Dienststelle Archive, Berlin, Germany. The United States transferred all POW records to POWs' home countries after World War II.

One of the pictures of Walter Schmid taken while he was at Camp Gruber, Oklahoma, in 1943. POWs could use their canteen coupons to pay for photographs like these to be made at the camp. Courtesy of Walter Schmid.

German POWs marching in formation through Camp McAlester, Oklahoma, ca. early 1944. Courtesy of Walter Schmid.

The band in Walter Schmid's *Afrika Korps* unit marching at
Camp McAlester, Oklahoma, ca. early 1944. The entire band was
shipped together to the United States as POWs.
Courtesy of Walter Schmid.

Headquarters building of Camp Las Cruces as it appeared in
the period between its use as a Civilian Conservation Corps
(CCC) camp and as a POW camp, ca. early 1940s.
Courtesy of P. H. Beckett, COAS Publishing & Research Files,
Las Cruces, New Mexico.

Barracks at Camp Las Cruces (with the headquarters in the background), ca. early 1940s. Courtesy of P. H. Beckett, COAS Publishing & Research Files, Las Cruces, New Mexico.

Military portrait of Captain Clark Williams, commander of Camp Las Cruces during much of Schmid's stay there. Courtesy of Mark Williams, Indianapolis, Indiana.

Franz Ertl, another German POW held at Camp Las Cruces, whom Schmid knew. Courtesy of Walter Schmid.

Fritz Kehrer, a fellow German POW from Camp Las Cruces, who was the camp spokesman. Courtesy of Walter Schmid.

A group photograph of German POWs at Camp Gruber, Oklahoma, all still wearing either their German or *Afrika Korps* uniforms. Fritz Kehrer, whom Walter Schmid knew at Camp Gruber and Camp Las Cruces, is second from the left in the front row.
Courtesy of Walter Schmid.

German POW
Gert Kissinger served
as a translator at
Camp Las Cruces.
Courtesy of
Walter Schmid.

A wartime photograph of Junior Barela, a Mexican field worker whom Schmid met at Stahmann Farm. Courtesy of Walter Schmid.

On one occasion the photographer visiting Camp Las Cruces brought clothing props. Schmid posed for this picture wearing a Mexican sombrero. Courtesy of Walter Schmid.

Felipe Guzman, one of the
Mexican field workers whom
Schmid met during the war,
in 1998 when Schmid
visited him in Las Cruces.
Courtesy of Walter Schmid.

Walter Schmid and Sally Rovirosa, granddaughter of Dean
Stahmann, who employed Schmid as a POW. The pecan fields
in the background were either fields of cotton or newly
planted trees in the mid-1940s when Schmid worked there.
Courtesy of New Mexico Farm and Ranch Heritage Museum.

In 1999 Walter Schmid met Hans Rudi Poethig, a former German POW held at Camp Roswell, and Toshi Nakayama. Schmid worked at the Nakayama farm north of Las Cruces and recalls the then very young Toshi from his days there. Courtesy of New Mexico Farm and Ranch Heritage Museum.

A recent picture of Walter Schmid and his wife, Marta, with whom he corresponded during the war. Courtesy of Walter and Marta Schmid.

Schmid during the period he was a post-war POW in England, ca. 1947. Courtesy of Walter Schmid.

Epilogue

by Robert L. Hart

Curator and Exhibit Project Director of
"To Get the Job Done" New Mexico Farm and
Ranch Heritage Museum, Las Cruces, New Mexico

Walter Schmid continued to play trumpet after the war for his church trumpet ensemble, eventually becoming the group leader. He also continued to work as a toolmaker at the same firm he left before being drafted during World War II (and from which he retired in 1985). He married his wartime girlfriend and correspondent, the former Marta Pflueger. He and Marta have two children. His manuscript was written to explain his participation in World War II to his grandson, Stephan.

Having already returned to both England and North Africa at various times, Walter Schmid returned to Las Cruces during September 1998, seeking his former Spanish-speaking friends: Junior Barela, Willie and Philip Guzman, and Ernesto Padilla. By running a red light, he came to the attention of the Las Cruces police, who, with the aid of an interpreter, were able to help him in his search. Featured in a front-page article in the *Las Cruces Sun-News,* Walter thus came to the attention of the staff at the newly opened New Mexico Farm and Ranch Heritage Museum.

Museum staff were aware of POW use in the state during World War II. Initial research had not revealed, however, whether there was enough extant material, both human and artifactual, to mount an exhibit. Walter Schmid proved to be a veritable gold mine of information. He had a manuscript written for his family on his military service and had retained diaries from his captivity. He also had historic and recent photographs of African battlefields, as well as photos of himself and some of his fellow Las Cruces POWs. The museum became convinced that, with Walter's cooperation, an exhibit on POW use in agriculture was a real possibility.

During each of the next two years Walter returned to Las Cruces in the fall. During his second visit, Walter donated exhibit materials to the museum, which conducted extensive interviews with him. Walter was also introduced to another former German POW at Roswell, New Mexico—Hans Rudi Poethig, who had immigrated to the United States after the war. The two visited Stahmann Farm, the Nakayama farm, and the old headquarters building and site of the Melendres Street Las Cruces camp.

Between the second and third visits, Walter condensed his manuscript for the museum. The museum then had the manuscript translated by Dr. Richard Rundell of New Mexico State University. Exhibit team members first publicly presented papers during the annual Historical Society of New Mexico conference in Valencia County in 2000. After the panel session a member of the society's publication committee approached the museum about sponsoring a publication of the Schmid manuscript.

Walter Schmid no longer drives, but has made a fourth visit to New Mexico in order to see the "To Get the Job Done" exhibit for which he served as a catalyst. He also served as a field trip guide for the joint New Mexico–Arizona History Convention in Las Cruces during April 2002, revisiting the camp headquarters, Stahmann Farm, and the former Nakayama Farm. He has privately published a longer version of his manuscript in Germany under the title *Einer unter Vielen* [*One of Many*] (now in its second printing).

Grant support for the manuscript translation was received from the New Mexico Endowment for the Humanities. Conference attendance was made possible by grants from the Doña Ana County Historical Society. Additional support was provided by the New Mexico Farm and Ranch Heritage Foundation.

Epilogue

New Mexican readers who lived through World War II can take pride in their contributions to the war effort. Other New Mexican readers too young to remember World War II will be interested in learning about POW use in agriculture, a little-known home-front story.

———

Appendix

LAS CRUCES CAMP DIARY

Recorded by Walter Schmid • Translated by Richard Rundell

Four hundred men were transferred on 27 July 1944 by train from Camp Gruber, Oklahoma, to Las Cruces, New Mexico. The route was via Emporia and Newton, Kansas; Lamar & La Junta, Colorado; and Anajo and Socorro, New Mexico. We arrived in Las Cruces on 28 July 1944 at 2:00 PM We walked from the train station to what had previously been an Italian POW camp. It had no barbed wire.

JULY 1944

29	$3.00 advance; roll call for health check
30	Sunday
31	weeded cotton; at 1:30 farmer came & told us it wasn't worth it, brought us back to camp; there we were locked up allegedly for refusing to work; released after 3 hours

AUGUST 1944

1	chopped cotton
2	" "

3	" "
4	" " $16.50 handed in earlier was returned
5	" "
6	Sunday
7	" " movie (American film)
8	" " caught a rattlesnake
9	rainy weather dental exam
10	rainy weather
11	chopped cotton, 7 hours
12	" " 5 men ran away from subsidiary camp, caught again right away
13	Sunday
14	chopped cotton
15	" "
16	" "
17	" " wages $10.30
18	" "
19	" "
20	Sunday
21	chopped cotton
22	" "
23	" "
24	rainy weather
25	chopped cotton
26	" " due to regular mistreatment and threatened with beating, complaint to Red Cross
27	Sunday "PW" stenciled in red on all articles of clothing
28	chopped cotton health check; only penis examined
29	" "
30	" "
31	" "

Total of 24 workdays

SEPTEMBER 1944

1	chopped cotton
2	" "
3	Sunday

4	chopped cotton
5	" " all officers transferred
6	" " Völk (from Ulm) falls from car on Melendres St.
7	" "
8	" " Hitler salute introduced in German Army
9	" "
10	Sunday inoculation
11	chopped cotton
12	" "
13	" "
14	" " wages $22.00
15	rainy weather
16	rainy weather
17	Sunday
18	chopped cotton new arrivals; bunks stacked two high
19	" "
20	" "
21	beginning of cotton harvest, picked 60 lbs., paid 32¢
22	101 lbs., 61¢
23	97 lbs.
24	Sunday health check
25	126 lbs.
26	rainy weather
27	132 lbs.
28	106 lbs.
29	130 lbs.
30	132 lbs.

Total = 884 lbs.

OCTOBER 1944

1	Sunday
2	132 lbs.
3	131 lbs.
4	148 lbs. wages $20.35
5	147 lbs.
6	151 lbs. news from Red Cross that much mail has been lost

7	143 lbs.
8	Sunday
9	141 lbs.
10	151 lbs.
11	143 lbs.
12	132 lbs.
13	150 lbs. 3 men tried to escape last night; 80 newcomers
14	144 lbs.
15	Sunday
16	160 lbs. the 3 men were caught & brought back
17	158 lbs.
18	150 lbs.
19	157 lbs.
20	171 lbs.
21	164 lbs.
22	Sunday
23	180 lbs.
24	163 lbs.
25	165 lbs.
26	rainy weather went to dentist at Ft. Bliss
27	rainy weather
28	rainy weather
29	Sunday donated blood
30	146 lbs. belongings searched
31	149 lbs.

Total for October = 3,476 lbs.

NOVEMBER 1944

1	174 lbs.
2	168 lbs.
3	175 lbs.
4	180 lbs.
5	Sunday wage list $24.54
6	rainy weather
7	182 lbs. Flying Fortress flew low & dropped money bag for farmer
8	175 lbs. movie

136

9	171 lbs.
10	177 lbs.
11	170 lbs.
12	Sunday
13	170 lbs.
14	172 lbs.
15	177 lbs.
16	rainy day
17	rainy day
18	rainy day
19	Sunday 7 units had to work, cutting lettuce for farmer Nakayama, upper camp went on strike, kitchen & canteen closed
20	166 lbs.
21	177 lbs. movie
22	175 lbs. upper camp had to go back to work
23	177 lbs.
24	repaired fences for 6 hrs. for Mandel, trucked out manure
25	170 lbs.
26	Sunday
27	112 lbs. health check
28	170 lbs.
29	124 lbs.
30	150 lbs.

Total November = 3,512 lbs.

DECEMBER 1944

1	179 lbs.
2	176 lbs.
3	Sunday physical exam, placed in Group A
4	177 lbs.
5	192 lbs. movies
6	188 lbs.
7	178 lbs.
8	190 lbs.
9	79 lbs. Indian cotton
10	Sunday

11	80 lbs. Indian cotton
12	89 lbs.
13	182 lbs. Egyptian cotton
14	172 lbs.
15	173 lbs.
16	170 lbs.
17	Sunday
18	174 lbs.
19	160 lbs. 4 groups locked up for poor work, 2 without clothes, 2 outdoors for refusal to strip; one man beaten senseless by captain in closed room, driven off in closed car
20	189 lbs.
21	166 lbs. 2 groups locked up outdoors in short underpants
22	167 lbs. the 2 groups were released
23	180 lbs.
24	Sunday Christmas Eve, 10 AM health check, 3 PM military church service in Camp II
25	holiday 3 PM concert
26	rainy day
27	65 lbs. rain in the afternoon
28	rainy day Captain checked haircuts before supper; 80% locked up until they get hair cut shorter. I cut Franz's hair with my nail scissors, and he cut mine
29	rainy day
30	187 lbs.
31	Sunday An American officer insulted a POW with *Schweinehund* [literally = "pig dog"; probably "son of a bitch" in English]; captain takes reprisals against upper camp and officer

Total for December 1944 = 3,513 lbs.

JANUARY 1945

1	172 lbs.
2	177 lbs.
3	175 lbs.
4	172 lbs.
5	171 lbs.

6	176 lbs. group 14 in guardhouse
7	Sunday 20 men transferred to Ft. Bliss
8	172 lbs.
9	176 lbs.
10	174 lbs.
11	173 lbs.
12	258 lbs. bolls
13	102 lbs. bolls 3 hours, then broke corn stalks
14	Sunday went to soccer game in Camp II
15	158 lbs. 20 newcomers
16	180 lbs.
17	rainy day
18	179 lbs. movie
19	170 lbs.
20	172 lbs.
21	Sunday
22	176 lbs.
23	170 lbs.
24	186 lbs.
25	212 lbs.
26	25 lbs. rain
27	132 lbs.
28	Sunday health check
29	156 lbs.
30	153 lbs.
31	135 lbs.

Total for January 1945 = 4,302 lbs.

FEBRUARY 1945

1	in guardhouse due to too low work output
2	in guardhouse without food or water
3	in guardhouse
4	in guardhouse, released
5	187 lbs. in Camp II, a guard shot & killed a man as he climbed the fence as usual to fetch a ball
6	224 lbs.
7	210 lbs. burial of the man who was shot, Ft. Bliss

8	200 lbs.
9	188 lbs.
10	186 lbs.
11	Sunday
12	no work
13	no work, began English and shorthand classes
14	no work
15	" " new repressive measures used by American camp administration against us every day
16	no work
17	" "
18	Sunday
19	no work
20	" "
21	" " all underwear stenciled with "PW"
22	" "
23	" "
24	" "
25	Sunday
26	cleaned irrigation ditches
27	" "
28	work group 17 in guardhouse

Total February 1945 = 1,195 lbs.

MARCH 1945

1	work
2	work
3	work
4	Sunday
5	work
6	work Camp II was transferred and dissolved
7	work
8	work for farmer Dill
9	" "
10	work
11	Sunday

12	work guardhouse unit transferred outdoors
13	"
14	"
15	"
16	"
17	"
18	"
19	my birthday
20	
21	
22	Captain Williams asked for anti-Nazis; any such should write him a letter; no one wrote, so we were declared a Nazi Camp and all rights were taken away. Our camp leader had to guarantee order with his life; situation getting worse.
23	
24	
25	Sunday
26	
27	Red Cross representative visited us, later also a reporter
28	Franz Ertl transferred with 24 others
29	Hitler salute is prohibited, as well as all political photos [i.e. of Hitler]
30	We were photographed while eating

APRIL 1945
[no entries for this month]

MAY 1945

7	End of war
15	Whole camp went back to daily cotton chopping, weeding melons, picking melons; together with Junior Barela, Ernesto Padilla, & Philip Guzman

JUNE, JULY, AUGUST 1945
[no entries for these months]

SEPTEMBER 1945

[no entries for 1–17 September]

Cotton harvest began at Stahmann Farm

18	68 lbs. 4 hrs.
19	132 lbs. 8 hrs.
20	143 lbs.
21	100 lbs.
22	93 lbs.
23	Sunday health check
24	181 lbs.
25	198 lbs.
26	205 lbs.
27	201 lbs.
28	212 lbs.
29	209 lbs.
30	Sunday

Total for September 1945 = 1,742 lbs.

OCTOBER 1945

1	208 lbs.
2	25 lbs. rain
3	rain
4	200 lbs.
5	131 lbs. 3 1/2 hours
6	rain
7	209 lbs. Sunday
8	51 lbs. rain
9	"
10	"
11	"
12	219 lbs.
13	202 lbs.
14	227 lbs. Sunday
15	204 lbs.
16	207 lbs.
17	208 lbs.
18	206 lbs.

Appendix

19	215 lbs.
20	207 lbs.
21	Sunday
22	229 lbs.
23	211 lbs.
24	206 lbs.
25	217 lbs.
26	225 lbs.
27	231 lbs.
28	Sunday
29	220 lbs.
30	226 lbs.
31	223 lbs.

Total for October 1945 = 4,707 lbs.

NOVEMBER 1945

1	230 lbs.
2	240 lbs.
3	226 lbs.
4	Sunday
5	223 lbs.
6	225 lbs.
7	225 lbs.
8	228 lbs.
9	222 lbs.
10	227 lbs.
11	Sunday
12	215 lbs.
13	190 lbs.
14	199 lbs.
15	229 lbs.
16	207 lbs.
17	194 lbs.
18	Sunday
19	221 lbs.
20	221 lbs.
21	207 lbs.

22	Thanksgiving Day
23	213 lbs.
24	216 lbs.
25	Sunday clothing [laundry?] check
26	231 lbs.
27	221 lbs.
28	went to dentist at Ft. Bliss, overnight [in El Paso]
29	back to Las Cruces, with Georg Theurl
30	173 lbs. (208)

Total for November 1945 = 4,983 lbs.

DECEMBER 1945

1	170 lbs.
2	Sunday
3	267 lbs.
4	377 lbs.
5	172 lbs.
6	118 lbs.
7	179 lbs.
8	182 lbs.
9	Sunday
10	178 lbs.
11	190 lbs.
12	176 lbs. had my photo taken
13	176 lbs.
14	light snow during night, no work
15	316 lbs.
16	Sunday
17	316 lbs.
18	319 lbs.
19	267 lbs.
20	305 lbs.
21	308 lbs.
22	321 lbs.
23	Sunday health check
24	309 lbs.
25	holiday

26	305 lbs. end of shaving heads bald; groups 1 & 2 in guardhouse
27	246 lbs.
28	260 lbs.
29	280 lbs.
30	Sunday
31	176 lbs. wages $21.40

Total for December 1945 = 5,913 lbs.

JANUARY 1946

1	holiday
2	165 lbs.
3	164 lbs.
4	195 lbs.
5	124 lbs. rain
6	Sunday
7	rain
8	150 lbs.
9	snow
10	snow
11	198 lbs.
12	164 lbs.
13	Sunday
14	snow
15	"
16	"
17	201 lbs. bolls
18	rain
19	rain
20	Sunday
21	rain
22	138 lbs. bolls
23	155 lbs. b.
24	141 lbs. b.
25	134 lbs. b.
26	132 lbs. b.
27	Sunday

28   rain

29   no work

30   " "

31   " "   we were issued black uniforms

Total for January 1946 = 2,061 lbs.

FEBRUARY 1946

1   no work; clothes check; Deming camp stops here on
        their way to Ft. Bliss; Franz Ertl among them

2   no work

[Diary stops.]

Until our departure, I worked at Stahmann Farm hoeing, cleaning ditches, etc. together with Junior and Willie Barela, Ernesto Padilla, and Philip Guzman, four young Mexicans from Las Cruces and Mesilla.

12 March 1946—went by truck to Ft. Bliss

19 March—by train via Kansas [City] & Chicago to Camp Shanks, near New York

28 March—by train to New York City, boarded ship and departed for Europe

Instead of being released, used for reconstruction work in England.

July 1947—release home

———

WALTER SCHMID'S POEMS
WRITTEN IN LAS CRUCES, CIRCA 1945

Las Cruces

Beneath the southern sun's rays
surrounded by cotton fields and desert.
In the distance, mountains deserted and bare,
scarcely a bird sings in the air.

There lies Las Cruces dreamily in between,
an oasis in the Mexican land.
With its old lanes, houses, and niches
rarely mentioned and little known.

Loyal and industriously committed to their work,
in low houses, drafty and crooked
they live and lead a happy life,
Mexicans, called by the cotton.

—

The Rio Grande gives its water
to soak earth and sand,
since mercilessly the sun sends
its rays onto city and land.

The crosses chosen as its sign,
they testify of bloody battle.
Many Spaniards lost their lives
through the Indians' grim might.

Although little but cacti may bloom,
and rain may hardly dampen the fields
and many sandstorms pass over you.
Yet we want to commemorate
a monument to Las Cruces.

New Mexico

New Mexico, you land of delights,
the sun always laughs over you,
no rain brings you relief.
At night, the moon watches over you.

You land of unending expanses,
with sandy mesas and stony heights.
No winter brings you refreshment,
over your fields, only sandstorms blow.

No forests decorate your hills
No fresh springs to quench nature's thirst.
No joyful cries on mountain ridges,
the sun suffocates everything before it blooms.
The prairie lies still and abandoned,
the heat waves shimmer above the thorn bushes.
Where Indians once, in dances and games,
cooled their heated blood.

Where at night around the campfire's flames
the old songs rose to the sky
and redskins in harmony together
dreamt of great victories.

In the valleys near shallow rivers
where water sparingly nourishes the soil,
cotton fields grow and flourish,
wild animals make their way to the brook.

Towns and villages from earlier days,
white houses with low roofs.
Old customs, habits, and tales
keep old and young ever awake.

A place in the great land of the free,
free country with a wide view.

> Perhaps you'll also offer a newcomer
> Freedom, affluence, and happiness.

Walter Schmid wrote these two poems, "Las Cruces" and "New Mexico," while he was at Camp Las Cruces sometime in 1945. Translated by Richard Rundell.

———

RED CROSS INSPECTION REPORTS

WORK DETAIL OF LAS CRUCES, NEW MEXICO
Branch [camp] of Fort Bliss, Texas.

Visited by Mr. Métraux, 13 April 1945.

<u>Spokesman</u>: SIEPER, Rudy, Private First Class   8 WG–28089
Number of Men: 296   German Prisoners
                        2   members of Medical Personnel

<u>Location</u>

This camp, with a capacity of 300 men, is located in the Rio Grande del Norte valley, 60 kilometers northwest of El Paso, one of the large Texas cities. The region is healthy and very dry. The winters are cold and summers hot. The lack of humidity makes the region very comfortable. The fields are very fertile and the trees are very beautiful thanks to the large irrigation systems.

The [POW] camp is an old American labor camp, i.e. Civilian Conservation Corps, which was established during the Depression in order to provide work for the unemployed and develop new areas. The buildings are constructed of wood. They have one story, and despite their plainness, prove to be very comfortable.

<u>Lodgings</u>

The barracks of the prisoners are large and clean. Each barrack contains 40 POWs; there is sufficient air and light for all of them. The heating system generates hot air. Each barrack contains a large furnace that heats

M/JRh/AT

Etats-Unis d'Amérique

Copie conforme

ARCHIVES DU CICR

DETACHEMENT DE TRAVAIL DE LAS CRUCES, NEW MEXICO

(dépendant de Fort Bliss, Texas).

Visité par M. Métraux le 13 avril 1945.

Homme de confiance: SIEPER Rudy, "Obergefreiter" 8 WG-28089

Effectif: 296 prisonniers allemands
2 membres du Personnel Sanitaire.

Situation

Ce camp, d'une capacité de 300 hommes, est situé dans la
vallée du Rio Grande del Norte, à 60 kilomètres au nord-ouest de
El Paso, une des grandes villes du Texas. La région est salubre
et très sèche. Les hivers sont froids et les étés chauds. L'ab-
sence de toute humidité rend la région très agréable. Grâce à de
grands travaux d'irrigation, les champs sont très fertiles et les
arbres très beaux.

Le camp lui-même est un ancien camp d'ouvriers américains
du "Civilian Conservation Corps" - organisation créée pendant la
crise pour donner du travail aux chômeurs et développer de nou-
velles régions. Les bâtiments sont en bois, à un étage, et mal-
gré leur grande simplicité, peuvent être rendus très confortables.

Logements

Les baraques où vivent les prisonniers sont vastes et
propres. Elles contiennent chacune 40 prisonniers; il y a suf-
fisamment d'air et de lumière pour tous. Le chauffage se fait
à l'air chaud. Chaque baraque possède un grand appareil qui ré-
chauffe l'air et le distribue dans toute la baraque. Les prisonniers sont responsables des précautions contre les incendies;
ils disposent d'une pompe automatique et d'appareils extincteurs
chimiques. Chaque prisonnier a un lit en fer, avec des ressorts
en acier. La literie est bonne (deux couvertures très épaisses,
un matelas, et une taie d'oreiller).

L'homme de confiance possède plusieurs exemplaires de
la Convention de Genève en allemand et en anglais. Il n'est donc
pas nécessaire de l'afficher. Les ordres sont donnés en anglais
et traduits en allemand par un prisonnier.

**Copy of the first page of the original French-filed Red Cross
inspection report of Camp Las Cruces on April 13, 1945.
Archive of the International Red Cross, Geneva, Switzerland.**

the air and distributes it throughout the barrack. The POWs are responsible for the precaution against fires [fire safety drills]. They have an automatic pump and a chemical fire extinguisher available. Each POW has an iron bed with a steel spring. The bedding is good (two very thick covers, a mattress, and a pillow case).

The spokesperson has a number of copies of the Geneva Convention available, both in German and in English. He does not think it necessary to post them. The orders are given in English and then translated into German by one POW.

Sanitary installations

The camp contains two large privies, showers, [and] laundry facilities, where the POWs can always use hot water.

Food

The POWs prepare three meals per day. They receive ample portions (which resemble those that are distributed at Camp Fort Bliss) and prepare nutritious and appetizing menus.

The kitchen contains two large dining facilities (numerous gas stoves and two large refrigerators).

There has been no problem with regard to the food.

Medical care and hygiene

The infirmary, where primary treatment is offered and where light cases are being treated, is located several meters from the camp. The two members of the German medical personnel work there. A civilian physician from Las Cruces makes his medical rounds once per day. The sick soldiers are taken by ambulance to the base camp hospital in Fort Bliss.

On 4 February, the soldier Wolfgang SCHLEGEL was killed by an American soldier because he attempted to escape. This case is being reported to the Swiss legation by the American authorities.

Clothes

Each POW has all the necessary clothes:

Slacks	4 pairs,
shirts	2
jacket	1

overcoat	1
shorts	2 cotton, 2 wool,
undershirts	2 cotton, 2 wool,
socks	4 pairs
shoes	2 pairs
hats/caps	2

The uniforms and underwear are changed every three weeks. All the clothes resemble American uniforms (in quality and color).

The POWs have a laundry in the shower stalls. They can use as much soap as they need.

Money and pay

Since their capture, the German POWs have handed over their money against a receipt from the American authorities. That money is deposited in their account. Every month, the POWs receive their pay in the form of coupons to be used in the canteen. The amount they can keep is unlimited. The POWs are not permitted to send their money to their home country.

Work

The day starts at 6:30 AM (reveille). At 6:45 AM, first roll call, and at 7:00 AM breakfast. Those prisoners who work leave camp at 7:30 AM and start their work at 8:00 AM At noon, a second roll call, and immediately thereafter lunch is served. The work crews return to their work at 12:30 PM and work from 1:00 PM to 5:00 PM Dinner is served at 6:15 PM, immediately after the third roll call. The curfew is at 10:30 PM

At the day of our visit, only 60 POWs worked under contract. These men receive $0.80 per day for their work in the fields and irrigation channels. The work conditions and the governing labor laws of the POWs resemble those that are enforced for the civilian workers in the area. In case of an accident, the prisoner receives $0.40 per diem until his complete recovery. In that region, labor is not unhealthy and is not directly related to the war efforts of the United States.

Canteen

At the day of our visit, the canteen was closed on orders of the commandant based on a request by the [POWs'] spokesman. The reason was

Appendix

that the day before our visit, an inspection had taken place and the canteen was discovered to be dirty and untidy. The common penalty (shutting the canteen) was to last for three days. Nevertheless, we had the opportunity to look at the canteen's inventory. Just as at Fort Bliss, the base camp, the goods are sold at a much lower price than in the local economy. The canteen sells only items for everyday use (toilet accessories, items for artists, etc.).

The canteen's profits are used for the POWs (to buy sports articles, radios, etc.). The spokesman, in agreement with the spokesman of the base camp, makes the decision concerning the use of the canteen's funds.

The POWs can only rarely purchase cigarettes, but they can buy as much tobacco as they want. They roll their cigarettes with the help of small machines, which can be purchased at the canteen.

Religious services

There is no chaplain for the POWs. An American pastor of German origin comes from time to time to conduct a service for the Protestant POWs.

Free time and physical exercises

A sports area is located outside the camp. The POWs are only authorized to use it once a week for two hours. We asked the camp commandant to permit the POWs to use the area at least once a day. The commandant told us that this would be impossible due to the lack of guards. There are no other opportunities to engage in sports. The POWs may stay in the open as much as they want and play with the [soccer] ball on the streets of the camp's interior.

The camp library consists of 300 books in English and 150 books in German. The majority of these books were sent to the camp by the International Red Cross and the YMCA.

The POWs have established a fairly complete study program:
languages: English, French, Spanish, German
math
stenography
advertising
agriculture
mechanics

153

An orchestra consisting of eleven members presents concerts from time to time. One film is shown every month. Two radios will be purchased.

Correspondence

We will mention in our report to Fort Bliss, the base camp, details concerning the mail [service]. Letters and parcels for the POWs in this camp [Las Cruces] go through Fort Bliss.

Charity

As is the case in the base camp, a variety of supplies are distributed to this camp [Las Cruces] by the International Committee of the Red Cross and the YMCA.

Complaints

The spokesman of the base camp indicated to us that the penalties in this camp have been excessively harsh. We had the opportunity to interrogate a German POW who had been arrested during the day of our visit. We note the following:

1. The prison is some kind of a barbed-wire cage. One man can walk around there and can easily stand upright.
2. A POW who is faced with a disciplinary penalty is placed in this cage for one or two weeks based on the gravity of his offense. He only receives food every three days. The sole meal consists of two fried eggs, four slices of bread, and a bowl of vegetable soup.
3. The sentenced POW does not receive anything to read.
4. The sentenced POW does not get any blankets (covers) for the night and must sleep on the bare ground.

We have presented these facts to the camp commandant, who told us that unless he receives orders from his superiors, he will not change this method. We explained to him that this kind of punishment does not conform to the Geneva Convention and is also not permitted by American military law.

As the commandant categorically refused to modify his viewpoint, we submitted these facts to the commandant of the base camp (Fort Bliss).

The latter one assured us that measures will be taken to put an end to this kind of punishment.

We have concluded that the commandant of this camp had little sensitivity. When we told him that he must stop applying this kind of punishment, he mentioned to us that the POWs like him a lot. We have the impression that he does not comprehend the psychology of the POWs and that instead he has made enemies. That is what the spokesman told us. This is the first time in the United States that we have been confronted with such a situation.

We interrogated the spokesman and his aides without witnesses. These men talked to us very freely and with much confidence. We have to add that, on the subject of the commandant, the spokesman told us that he [the commandant] is also very strict with the American soldiers and that in most cases concerning discipline, the German POWs and the American guards receive the same treatment.

Translated from the original French to English by Wolfgang T. Schlauch.

———

WORK DETAIL OF LAS CRUCES, NEW MEXICO

Visited by Mr. Guy S. Métraux, accompanied by Mr. Eldon F. Nelson, from the State Department on 11 February 1946.

We visited the camp on 13 April 1945 and we submitted our report of 3 May 1945 in great detail concerning the general description, the interior setup, the sanitary installations, etc. In this report we will mention the changes.

The commandant is still Captain Clark J. Williams, with whom we had our last visit. A new section, which on all accounts resembles those described in our last report, has been added and the number of POWs has doubled. At the day of our visit there were:

POWs	Medical Staff	Total
NCOs: 49	—	49
Soldiers: 601	—	601
Total: 650	—	650 German POWs

The spokesman is still Private First Class Rudy Sieper, 8 WG–28089.

General Comments.

The general appearance of the camp has not changed. The buildings are well and properly kept. The sanitary installations are hygienic and comfortable. The food is good, the medical care is adequate. The doctor who comes to the camp is still the same and has the POWs' confidence.

Work.

At the day of our visit only 65 POWs worked in the fields (construction of the irrigation channels). The others waited for spring.

The daily schedule has changed little and is as follows:

Reveille:	06:15
Breakfast:	06:45
Lunch:	12:00
Dinner:	17:45
curfew:	22:30

The POWs work in the fields for nine hours (including one hour for lunch). One group of POWs works inside the POW camp: upkeep of the buildings, kitchen, etc. All those who work receive $0.80 per day.

Free Time: Sports, Education, etc.

We wrote in our last report: "The POWs are authorized to use the sports facility for only two hours once a week. We asked the captain, the camp's commandant, to permit the POWs to use this facility at least once a day." The commandant refused this privilege due to the lack of guards. We are delighted to mention that since our [last] visit, and based on our request to the commandant of the base camp, this situation has changed and the POWs can use the sports facility when they want to and after they obtain permission from the CDT.

The following courses are offered:

Course	Participants
English I	20 POWs
English II	15 POWs
English III (conversation)	20 POWs

Appendix

Spanish	5 POWs
French	6 POWs
American History	10 POWs

There are several radios in the camp and loudspeakers that enable the POWs to listen to recorded concerts, to lectures and news.

Once a week a movie is shown.

General Observations.

As pointed out in the previous camp report, the problem of punishment in this camp was a very serious one. We should mention that thanks to our direct intervention with the superior military authorities (as indicated in our report of 3 May 1945) the situation has changed considerably.

Not only has the prison (that small cage described in our report) been dismantled, not only do the prisoners receive food, but the number of penalties have been reduced considerably. The commandant has gained some of the POWs' trust and on the day of our visit there were no punishments. The spokesperson had no complaints and the camp was a model of order, and the morale was excellent.

We have here a typical case where an intervention by a delegate of the Committee of the International Red Cross has helped those men who had suffered due to the CDT's error of judgment.

The camp we had visited on 11 February 1945 [typo: should be 1946] cannot be compared to the camp we visited on 13 April 1945 in regard to morale and the general atmosphere.

Guy S. Métraux
Delegate

El Paso, Texas, 14 February 1946

Translated from the original French to English by Wolfgang T. Schlauch.

WALTER SCHMID'S PAY RECORD

PW CAMP ....FORT BLISS, TEXAS....

INDIVIDUAL PRISONER OF WAR PAY RECORD

SCHMID, WALTER	8WG 15990	Pvt.	5/11/43	10
Name	Serial No.	Rank	Date of Custody by U. S.	PW CO.

RECORD OF ALLOWANCES DUE

Date	Jan	Feb	Mar	Apr	May	Jun	Jul	Aug	Sep	Oct	Nov	Dec
1	1.08					-.80		-.80	-.80	1.08	1.20	-.80
2	1.16		-.80			-.80	-.80	-.80		-	1.20	
3	1.N			-.80			-.80	-.80		-.52	1.20	-.77
4	1.09					-.80	-.80	-.80	-.80	1.-		1.03
5	1.13	-.55				-.80	-.80		-.80	1.20	-.82
6	1.11	-.90				-.80	-.80	-.80	-.80	-	1.20	-.58
7		-.76				-.80	-.80	-.80	-.80	-.84	1.20	-.79
8	1.08	-.81	-.80		-.80	-.80		-.80	-.80	-	1.20	1.02
9	1.11	-.75	-.80		-.80	-.80	-.80			-	1.20	
10	1.10	-.74				-.80	-.80	-.80	-.80	1.20	-.88
11	1.09				-.80	-.80	-.80		-.80	1.15	1.10
12	1.13	-.80	-.80	-.80	-.80	-.80	-.80	1.19	1.15	-.96
13	-.91	-.80		-.80	-.80	-.80	-.80	1.02	-.90	-.96
14		-.80	-.80	-.80	-.80	-.80	1.20	-.89
15	-.89	-.80	-.80	-.80	-.65	-.80	1.06	1.20	-.93
16	1.14	-.80	-.80	-.80	-.80	1.07	1.07
17	1.13	-.80	-.80	-.80	-.80	-.80	1.08	-.94	-.94
18		-.80	-.80	-.80	-.80	1.06		-.96
19	1.08		-.80	-.80	-	-.80	1.N	1.20	-.89
20	1.10		-.80	-.80	-.80	-.80	1.07	1.11	-.92
21		-.80	-.80	-.80	-.80	1.07	-.92
22	1.02	-.80	-.80	-.80	-.80	1.20	-.92	-.96
23	1.05	-.80	-.80	-.80	-.80	1.11	1.13
24	-.79	-.80	-.80	-.80	-.81	1.06	1.16	-.96
25	-.15	-.80	-.80	-.80	-.88	1.17
26	-.09	-.11	-.80	-.80	-.80	1.05	1.26	1.20	-.8
27	-.51	-.10		-.80	-.80	-.80	1.01	1.20	1.20	-.75
28			-.80	-.80	-.80	1.12	21.17	-	-.76
29	-.66		-.80	-.80	-.80	-.80	1.19	1.20	-	-.70
30	-.63	-.80	-.80	-.80	-.80	-.80	1.20	1.08	
31	-.54		-.80		-.80	-.80		1.20	-.73
Total Work Allowance	21.76	6.18	8.-	4.80	16.-	20.80	20.80	21.45	20.56	24.77	27.12	21.44
Monthly Allowance	3.-	3.-	3.-	3.-	3.-	26	26.18	24	23	24	24	24
Total	24.76	9.18	11.-	7.80	19.-	20.80	20.80	21.45	20.56	24.77	27.12	21.44
*Adjustments												
Trust Fund					16.-	17.80	17.80	18.45	15.56	18.77	19.12	13.44
Coupons Authorized			7.80	8.-	3.-	3.-	3.-	5.-	6.-	8.-	8.-
PW Co Comdr Initials	RDB	RDB	GW	GW	GW		GA	BW		BW	GW
PW Initials	W.S.	W.S.	W.S.	W.S.	W.S.	W.S.	W.S.	W.S.	W.S.	W.S.	W.S.	WS
Voucher No.	36198	41367	46100	51918	47	5384						

*EXPLANATION OF ADJUSTMENTS AND REMARKS:

_____

_____

_____

8&C I-S 8&I Form No. 9
(Jan 45)

(USE OTHER SIDE FOR ADDITIONAL REMARKS)
(OVER)

This record shows how often Walter Schmid worked and how much he was paid. An interesting comparison can be made by comparing these notations with his diary entries for the work he did on each day. From the U.S. Army's POW reports for Schmid in the Deutsche Dienststelle Archive, Berlin, Germany. The United States transferred all POW records to the POWs' home countries after World War II.

WALTER SCHMID'S LETTERS TO MARTA

Translated by Wolfgang T. Schlauch

6 November 1943

Dear Marta!

It soon will be Christmas again and I am again far away from home. We will celebrate it, nevertheless. I wonder whether I can celebrate next Christmas again with you? Let us hope. Last Sunday our camp held Communion Services; it was well organized. Incidentally, this was the first sip of wine I had since Africa. A Sergeant Wolf from Niefern near Pforzheim received a letter from home some days ago. Dear Marta, how are you doing these days? You are and will always remain the same for me. Though we are separated by 8,000 kilometers, our thoughts bridge this distance, and one of these days this era will also pass.

Presently, we are only working two days during the week. We receive 80 cents for each working day. The weather is still very nice. However, it gets quite cold during the night.

I wish you a Merry Christmas and a Happy New Year. May it grant us our reunion.

With kindest regards,

Yours, Walter.

Camp Gruber, Oklahoma

America, June 26, 1944

My dear Marta!

For some time now I have been back in the camp. I am presently working in a military cemetery. I have not received mail for a long time. As always, I am healthy and sprightly, but I will be much more cheerful once I will be home again and am able to appreciate your presence. [Blocked out by censor] . . . I have not received any mail from your parents, a fact I don't like at all as you can imagine, particularly since I have written several times. The least I would have expected is that my letters would have been answered. Today, with faithful love, with kindest regards from Your Walter.

Camp Gruber, Prisoner of War Camp [Oklahoma]

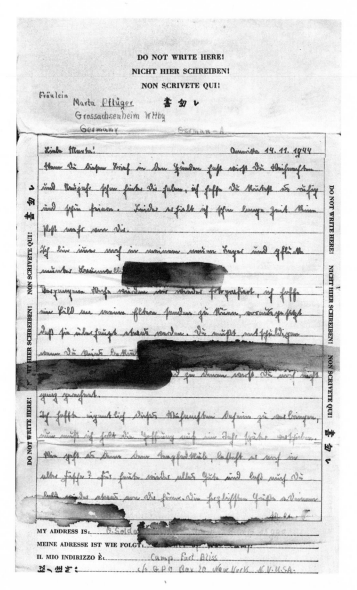

Walter Schmid corresponded regularly with his girlfriend, Marta.
The letters he saved include censorship stamps (both American and
German) and black crossed-out blocks where material was censored. They are written on the standard POW letter form, which
has instructions in several languages. Walter and Marta married
after he was returned to Germany. Courtesy of New Mexico Farm
and Ranch Heritage Museum, Las Cruces, New Mexico.

Appendix

My dear Marta!

And once again Christmas is just around the corner and again we will have to celebrate it being separated. I hope that you can spend it in the old traditional way. It will be very busy for you this time of the year. I was informed of the death of Walter Ziegler. This will be a major loss for Gertrud. You see, I am informed about several events. As always, I am feeling fine, I am always healthy and sprightly. We pick cotton every day, which, however, causes a great deal of backache.

I receive mail regularly. However, I have not received any from you for some time. We are allowed to send one letter and one postcard per week.

My mother wrote me that you have to work very hard. I hope that you will survive the strain. If you work on something where you have to bend heavily, then also think of me. I wish you and your parents a Merry Christmas. Maybe you can play again with the train. And a Healthy New Year. In faithful love, kindest regards, Your Walter.
Prisoner of War Camp, Fort Bliss [Las Cruces]

America, 11/14/1944

Dear Marta

When you receive this letter, you will have Christmas and New Year's behind you. I hope that you were able to celebrate it quietly and nicely. Unfortunately, I have not received any mail from you for a long time.

I am still in my camp and constantly pick cotton. [sentence blocked out by censor].

Last week, photos were again taken of us. I hope I can send a photo to my parents assuming that the photos will turn out all right. Please excuse me if you don't get any. . . [two lines blocked out by censor] . . . you are not yet part of them.

I actually hoped to spend this Christmas at home. Now, I must postpone this hope for another year. How are you doing with your [horse?] club; is it still very much alive?

All the best to you today and I hope to hear from you soon again. With kindest regards, from your Walter.
Fort Bliss [Las Cruces]

LETTER FROM
COUNCILLOR H. HANDFORD

Wandsworth Trades Council & Borough Labour Party
FOUNDED 1904

Treasurer and Asst. Secretary:
Councillor F. E. McKAY,
138 Earlsfield Road, S.W.18.
Telephone: BATTERSEA 4993.

President:
Councillor J. G. DEVINE.

General Secretary:
Councillor H. HANDFORD,
47 Tilehurst Road, S.W.18.
Telephone: BATTERSEA 8231.

INDUSTRIAL SECTION:
Chairman: Councillor J. G. DEVINE.
Secretary: Councillor F. E. McKAY.

POLITICAL SECTION:
Chairman: E. G. HICKS.
Secretary: Councillor H. HANDFORD.

TO WHOM ALL CORRESPONDENCE
MUST BE ADDRESSED.

Mr Walter Schmid.
Grossachsenheim. Germany.

8 November 1947

Dear Walter,

       I need hardly say how grateful I was to receive your letter dated 29 October, 1947, which came to me unopened and uncensored and I am replying to you per return of post. Well let me say that your thanks were greatly appreciated, and I also must say in return that I too thank you and your comrades for the easy time you gave me, whilst I was carrying out my job as one in charge. You all worked well, and I do not remember any occasion when I had the need to complain. I am glad too, that you found everything in order when you arrived home, also to know that your girl friend has been loyal and have awaited for you to return, and now that you are engaged, I trust you will be happy, and that this will continue throughout your life.

       Now Walter, I want you to take what I have to say in a kindly manner, because I realise as much as you, what I have to say will be to the point and it may hurt. You know me well enough to understand that it is against all my principles to deliberately hurt anyone , but it is best to be just, and sometimes justice is misunderstood.

       I note that the latter part of your letter seems embittered and that you are complaining of the treatment of your peoples and that they only sneer at our "democracy" and that many are tending to the left."Communism". I know that as a youth you came directly under the decade of Hitler when it appeared to the outside world that he was teaching hate , and it appears that you too have not yet rid yourself of this soul destroying evil. I thought that my talks to you would have given you an insight into the outlook of the British People their habit and character, and I rather hoped that my example would have convinced you of the sincerity of purpose and the desirability of good will to all peoples, and it does appear that I have failed. Now as regards the dismantling of your factories, let us both look at the position. Twice during 30 years Germany threw the world into a blood bath, twice they have been beaten, in the first world war this Country alone lost over a million Dead, countless homes were destroyed and broken up, familes rendered assunder, and wherever one looked devastation was rife. I was one of the first to advocate that the Rhur Valley should be given back to Germany, I believed then that Germany had been taught a lesson and that she would live in peace with her neighbours and the world generally. Well I must say that my beliefs were groundless and foolish, and the advent of Hitler and consequental happenings, has proved to the world that Germany is incabable of control and before she is given her place amongst the nations she must be re-educated

Appendix

Wandsworth Trades Council & Borough Labour Party
FOUNDED 1904

Treasurer and Asst. Secretary:
Councillor F. E. McKAY,
138 Earlsfield Road, S.W.18.
Telephone: BATTERSEA 4993.

President:
Councillor J. G. DEVINE.

General Secretary:
Councillor H. HANDFORD,
47 Tilehurst Road, S.W.18.
Telephone: BATTERSEA 8231.

INDUSTRIAL SECTION:
Chairman: Councillor J. G. DEVINE.
Secretary: Councillor F. E. McKAY.

POLITICAL SECTION:
Chairman: E. G. HICKS.
Secretary: Councillor H. HANDFORD.

TO WHOM ALL CORRESPONDENCE
MUST BE ADDRESSED.

and must prove herself capable of understanding the principles of Human rights and that all peoples whatever race creed or colour have the same right to live in peace without molestation from anyone. Think what Hitler did to London, try and remember that in 1940 when this Country stood alone, Hitler knowing the weakness of our air force launched an allout attack on the defenceless population and indescriminately dropped bombs,rendering many hundreds homeless and murdering hundreds. For over two months he kept this up, but to his amazement instead of weakening our morale he only made the incentive for us to go all out and beat him. In the Borough of Wandsworth we had some 70000 Houses totally destroyed or damaged by such action, to be exact. 16000 totally destroyed, 35000 badly damaged and 19000 damaged, and at the end of hostilities we had some 45000 homeless. This is only one part of London, many other parts suffered with equal severity, and even as I write we have still some 20000 persons still awaiting homes. I know our retaliation to many of your towns and cities became much worse than we ourselves suffered, but if any Country desires War they must expect their opponent to defend their own country will the same zeal as the attacker, and the loser should not complain, especially if the attacker is the loser, as was in the case of Germany. I write all this only to prove to you that the whole blame for the War was Germany, no other Country wanted or desired such a conflict, and now it is all over, all we in this Country desire to live in peace with all nations,and in order that Germany hhall be prevented from again breaking this peace we are determined that such preventitive measures as curbing the number of factories shall be used. You know Walter, that if a child plays with fire he get burnt, and he suffers, but in order to protect him from himself, it becomes necessary for the parents to put a guard around the fire. I think in this little parable you will see the whole trend of my argument. We in this Country do not wish to spite you, we are helping all we can,for you to get on your feet again, but you must help yourselves as well, and if you donot get all you want you should accept the position,and make the most of what you have. We in this Country are not getting all we want, we too are suffering, such is the evil of all Wars, but we are big enough to accept without complaint, and I think you should advise your people to do the same. One last point, you say the people are laughing at Democracy- well that is understood because they have so long ingnored their responsibility of political and social duties that they have lost the real meaning of democracy, and we are doing our best to create a better understanding especially with the younger generation, of the working of a true democracy which we pray and hope will put a new Germany amongst the Nations of the World.

I end this political discussion here.

After the war, Walter Schmid corresponded with H. Hanford, a councillor and General Secretary of the British Labour Party. This response casts some light on Schmid's feelings of the time and offers a British perspective on the rebuilding of Germany. Courtesy of Walter Schmid.

Bibliography

BOOKS

Billinger, Robert D., Jr. *Hitler's Soldiers in the Sunshine State: German POWs in Florida*. Gainesville: University of Florida Press, 2000.

Bischof, Günter, and Stephen E. Ambrose, eds. *Eisenhower and the German POWs: Facts against Falsehood*. Baton Rouge: Louisiana State University Press, 1992.

Carlson, Lewis H. *We Were Each Other's Prisoners: An Oral History of World War II*. New York: Basic Books, 1977.

Eriksen, Heino R. *The Reluctant Warrior: Former German POW Finds Peace in Texas*. Austin, Tex.: Eakin Press, 2001.

Fiedler, David. *The Enemy Among Us. POWs in Missouri during World War II*. St. Louis: Missouri Historical Society Press, 2003.

Gansberg, Judith M. *Stalag, U.S.A.: The Remarkable Story of German POWs in America*. New York: Crowell, 1977.

Hörner, Helmut. *A German Odyssey: The Journal of a German Prisoner of War*. Golden, Colo.: Fulcrum Pub., 1991.

Keefer, Louis E. *Italian Prisoners of War in America, 1941–1946: Captives or Allies?* New York: Praeger, 1992.

Koop, Allen V. *Stark Decency: German Prisoners of War in a New England Village*. Hanover, N.H.: University Press of New England, 1988.

Krammer, Arnold P. *Nazi Prisoners of War in America.* Lanham, Md.:
    Scarborough House, 1996.

Lewis, George G., and John Mewha. *History of Prisoner of War Utilization
    by the United States Army: 1776–1945.* Washington, D.C.:
    Department of the Army, 1955.

Maschke, Erich, ed. *Zur Geschichte der deutschen Kriegsgefangenen des
    Zweiten Weltkriegs; Vol. X/1: Die deutschen Kriegsgefangenen in
    amerikanischer Hand-USA,* by Hermann Jung. Bielefeld: Verlag
    Gieseking, 1972.

Moore, Bob and Kent Fedorowich, eds. *Prisoners of War and their Captors
    in World War II.* Oxford: Berg, 1996.

Overmans, Rudiger. *Soldaten hinter Stacheldraht. Deutsche Kriegsgefangene
    des Zweiten Weltkriegs.* Berlin and Munich: Propyläen, 2000.

Overmans, Rudiger, and Günter Bischof, eds. *Kriegsgefangenschaft im
    Zweiten Weltkrieg: Eine vergleichende Perspektive.* Ternitz-Pottschach:
    G. Hoeller, 1999.

Parnell, Wilma, with Robert Taber. *The Killing of Corporal Kunze.*
    Secaurus, N.J.: L. Stuart, 1981.

Powell, Allan K. *Splinters of a Nation: German Prisoners of War in Utah.*
    Salt Lake City: University of Utah Press, 1989.

Robin, Ron. *Barbed Wire College: Reeducating German POWs in the United
    States During World War II.* Princeton, N.J.: Princeton University
    Press, 1995.

Schlauch, Wolfgang. *In amerikanischer Kiiegsgefangenschaft. Berichte deutscher
    Soldaten aus dem Zweiten Weltkrieg.* 2nd rev. ed. Crailsheim: Baier
    Verlog, 2004.

Smith, Arthur L. *The War for the German Mind: Reeducating Hitler's
    Soldiers.* Providence, R.I.: Berghahn Books, 1996.

Spiller, Harry, ed. *Prisoners of Nazis: Accounts by American POWs in World
    War II.* Jefferson, N.C.: McFarland, 1998.

Sullivan, Mathew B. *Thresholds of Peace: Four Hundred Thousand German
    Prisoners and the People of Britain, 1944–1948.* London: H.
    Hamilton, 1979.

Walker, Richard P. *The Lone Star and the Swastika. German Prisoners of
    War in Texas.* Austin, Tex.: Eakin Press, 2001.

Bibliography

ARTICLES

Doyle, Frederick, J. "German Prisoners of War in the Southwest United States During World War II: An Oral History." Ph.D. thesis, University of Denver, 1978.

Doyle, Susan Badger. "German and Italian Prisoners of War in Albuquerque, 1943–1946." *New Mexico Historical Review* 66 (July 1991): 327–40.

Krammer, Arnold. "German Prisoners of War in the United States." *Military Affairs* 40 (April 1976): 68–73.

MacKenzie, Simon P. "The Treatment of Prisoners of War in World War II." *Journal of Modern History* 66 (September 1946): 487–520.

Rundell, Walter, Jr. "Paying the POW in World War II." *Military Affairs* 22 (Fall 1958): 121–34.

Schlauch, Wolfgang T. "Harvesting the Crops: Axis Prisoners of War and their Impact on Dona Ana County During World War II." *Southern New Mexico Historical Review* 9 (January 2002): 30–37.

Spidle, Jake W., Jr. "Axis Invasion of the American West: POWs in New Mexico, 1942–1946." *New Mexico Historical Review* 49 (April 1974): 93–122.

Wiggers, Richard D. "The United States and the Denial of Prisoner of War (POW) Status at the End of the Second World War." *Militärgeschichtliche Mitteilungen* 52 (1993): 91–104.

FILM AND VIDEO

History Undercover: Nazi POWs in America. Produced by the History Channel. 50 min. A&E Television Networks, 2002. Videocassette.

Soldaten hinter Stacheldraht [Soldiers Behind Barbed Wire]. Produced by German ARD television. 3 hours. German ARD television, 2000. Videocassette.

U.S. Army. *Handling Prisoners of War.* Training film produced by the U.S. Army. Approximately 28 min. U.S. Army, ca. 1943. 16mm film.